THE GAME WE KNEW

THE GAME
WE KNEW

HOCKEY IN THE FIFTIES

Mike Leonetti

Photography by Harold Barkley

RAINCOAST BOOKS

Vancouver

For my wife, Maria

First published in 1997 by
Raincoast Books
8680 Cambie Street
Vancouver, B.C.
v6p 6m9
(604) 323-7100

1 3 5 7 9 10 8 6 4 2

CANADIAN CATALOGUING IN PUBLICATION DATA

Leonetti, Mike, 1958-
The game we knew

ISBN 1-55192-111-1

1. National Hockey League – History. 2. National Hockey League – History –
Pictorial works. I. Barkley, Harold. II. Title.

GV847.8.N3L46 1997   796.962'64   c97-910455-6

Printed and bound in China through Palace Press International

Contents

Foreword by Johnny Bower *vi*

Introduction 1

Photographs 6

Afterword 118

Acknowledgements 120

Foreword

When the New York Rangers drafted me from the Cleveland Barons for the 1953-54 season, I had already spent eight years in the American Hockey League (AHL). I had played well there for a pretty successful team. Many people don't know that Cleveland was almost accepted into the National Hockey League (NHL) in 1952 and only lost out due to some last-minute financial snags. I played with and against many past and future NHL players in the AHL, so I knew I could compete with the big leaguers. Unfortunately there were only six goaltending jobs available in the NHL during the 1950s (and no back-ups!). I had no choice but to keep working hard and hope for a break, which finally came with the Rangers.

I was grateful for the opportunity and ended up playing in all 70 games that year, recording five shutouts to go along with 29 wins and 10 ties. But we missed the playoffs, and the man I replaced, Gump Worsley, regained his job the next season, and it was back to the minors for me. I knew Gump and the Rangers' management didn't always get along, so I was hopeful that I might get another shot. However, I was only recalled when Worsley was injured. Otherwise I played for Vancouver in the Western Hockey League (WHL) in 1954-55 before returning to the AHL with the Providence Reds the following year. Two years later I was back in Cleveland. I hadn't given up on the NHL, but I was getting older and time was running out.

Then I caught a break. During the 1958 playoffs, I was playing for the Barons and we had a great seven-game series against the Springfield Indians, who were coached by George "Punch" Imlach. Watching in the stands was Toronto Maple Leaf coach Billy Reay. The Leafs must have been impressed because they drafted my playing rights in June 1958 and offered me a two-year contract. As much as I wanted to play in the NHL, I was only going to give it a try if I could be assured of returning to Cleveland if things didn't work out in Toronto. I enjoyed playing for the Barons, and I had an off-season job at a factory all lined up. Only when the Cleveland owner, Mr.

Hendy, gave me the proper assurances did I say yes to the Leafs' offer. I never did end up going back.

The Leafs really wanted me for only two years while some of their young prospects, like Gerry Cheevers, developed in their system. But when Imlach took over as coach of the Leafs, he installed a tight defensive system, and solid rear guards like Allan Stanley and Tim Horton made life easier for the goalies. We started to win, and Punch, because he was very loyal to veteran players who performed for him, stuck with me in the net. I always worried about keeping my job, but I managed to fight off the competition and finally achieved my childhood dream of having my name engraved on the Stanley Cup. I never made a lot of money, but the Leafs treated me well, and I'll take four Stanley Cups anytime. They wanted me for a couple of years and I ended up staying for a decade.

Another person who proved he belonged in the NHL was photographer Harold Barkley. A very talented man in his own right, Barkley changed the way hockey was photographed. His work captured the action and the spirit of this great era of hockey. I get a kick out of seeing myself as a Ranger because most people remember me as a Maple Leaf. It's one of Barkley's photos that people ask me to autograph most often. There were many photos taken of me, but the ones done by Barkley seem to be those that are best remembered. As you look through this book, I'm sure you will see why this is true.

Johnny Bower
Mississauga, Ontario
May 1997

Introduction

The 1952 Stanley Cup semifinal between Montreal and Boston was a hard-hitting affair throughout. On April 8, in a seventh-game showdown at the Montreal Forum, the series was finally decided. In the second period of that contest Montreal star Maurice "Rocket" Richard was crunched between Boston's Bill Quackenbush and Leo Labine. As he lay crumpled on the ice, Richard's head was contorted in such a way that it appeared as if his neck were broken, and blood flowed from a nasty forehead gash. Richard retired to the dressing room, taking six stitches to close the cut, but was still groggy. The Rocket was used to taking a great deal of punishment – every great goal scorer does – but it looked as if this hit might end his night and the season for the Canadiens.

Somehow Richard got back to the Montreal bench in the late minutes of the third period, even though he had been discouraged from doing so. When he was told that the score was tied 1-1, he turned to coach Dick Irvin and let him know he was ready to play. Irvin saw an opportunity to unleash his greatest weapon, but he had reservations about Richard's condition. He also knew there was no point trying to hold Richard back, so he nodded at the Rocket.

That was all Richard needed. He was on the ice instantly to take a pass from teammate Emile "Butch" Bouchard near\his own net. From there he began a long solo trek, eluding an initial forechecker as he rushed the puck straight up the middle of the rink. He weaved his way past two other Bruins before reaching the Boston blue line where rear guards Quackenbush and Bob Armstrong waited for him. As he gathered speed, Richard tried to go outside of Quackenbush, but the Bruin veteran lunged to angle the Rocket into the corner.

By now Richard could smell a goal, and he made a sharp cut toward the Bruins' net, using his arm to ward off Quackenbush. Armstrong, meanwhile, was unable to get back into the action. Now in overdrive, Richard bore in on Boston goalie "Sugar" Jim Henry. Ironically Henry had also been hurt earlier in the game (a broken nose and two black eyes), but he had remained in the net and awaited the inevitable confrontation against Richard.

Maurice Richard always made sure he was ready for the Stanley Cup playoffs. He once held the record for most career playoff goals with 82. This mark ranked him sixth all-time as of the start of the 1997 playoffs. He still holds the record for most goals in the finals with 34.

Henry went down and stacked his pads, hoping to block a shot, but the Rocket quickly shifted the puck from his backhand to his forehand and deposited the disk in the far side of the net with his last ounce of energy.

The Forum crowd went wild as Richard was mobbed by his teammates. Practically semiconscious, the Rocket had given Montreal a 2-1 lead; a 3-1 final score ensured the Canadiens would go to the finals. At the end of the game, the still-bloody Richard shook hands with the black-and-blue Henry, two warriors who had been through a war sharing a quiet moment of mutual respect.

Most fans would agree that only the Rocket could score such a goal. While playing for hockey's greatest team, Richard would amass 82 playoff goals in his career. The 1950s belonged to the Montreal Canadiens, who won a total of six Stanley Cups, the last five consecutively between 1955 and 1960. Led by the Rocket (the first player to record 50 goals in a season and 500 in a career), the Canadiens piled up Stanley Cups, major trophies, and all-star berths year after year. Jacques Plante, Doug Harvey, Elmer Lach, Bert Olmstead, Dickie Moore, Jean Beliveau, and Bernie Geoffrion all had a hand in the new standards for goals, assists, points, and goals against that the Canadiens set. Some of their marks have never been equalled while others were only surpassed many years later in the postexpansion era.

But make no mistake, it was Richard who spearheaded the Canadiens' amazing success (how many people have a riot named after them?), and if he was missing, as he was in the 1955 playoffs, the team wasn't the same. In fact, in 1940 the Canadiens were in deep trouble and almost went out of business. But largely thanks to the arrival of the Rocket in the 1942-43 season the team was reborn and the franchise's fortunes revived. Under Richard's leadership the Canadiens reached new heights of excellence that present-day Habs still try to emulate. Despite their unparalleled success in the 1950s, though, the Canadiens did have a strong contender to battle for the league title year after year, and Richard had a rival who might have been his equal or better.

The Detroit Red Wings were playing the New York Rangers on February 1, 1959, at Madison Square Garden. The Rangers had a defenceman named Lou Fontinato, who fancied himself the NHL's heavyweight champ in this rough, physical era of hockey. The Ranger tough guy had fought with the Red Wings' man of steel, Gordie Howe, on previous occasions, including a stick battle, and was primed that night for a fight to settle any doubts about the league's strongman title. A player with a mean disposition, by his own admission, Howe knew Fontinato would be looking for him. Gordie never forgot his enemies, nor did he forgive them.

A scuffle broke out between the Red Wings' Red Kelly and the Rangers' Eddie Shack, and Howe moved in to help his teammate. He hit Shack with his stick, which brought Fontinato galloping to the rescue. As the two combatants faced each other, Howe grabbed Fontinato's sweater and pounded the Ranger's face repeatedly. One shot, in particular, busted Leapin' Louie's nose all over his face, causing blood to spurt everywhere. The Ranger brawler fought back and managed to cut Howe slightly while inflicting a black eye, but it was clear who the winner was. When other players saw how badly Fontinato was beaten, Howe never had to fight again.

Of course, Gordie Howe was much more than a fighter. He was, in fact, hockey's most durable, productive, and strongest performer for many years. Howe was the ultimate "power forward" before the term was coined. The big right winger won the Art Ross Trophy four years in a row (1951 to 1954) and became the league's most dominating goal scorer with seasons of 43, 47, and 49 goals. The Red Wings also became a league power by winning four Stanley Cups in the 1950s. Sid Abel, Ted Lindsay, Terry Sawchuk, Red Kelly, Bob Goldham, Marty Pavelich, and Tony Leswick all played significant roles in making the Motor City team almost the equal of the Canadiens. Howe, Lindsay, and Sawchuk set career marks that remained intact for years. In Sawchuk's case, his 103 shutouts (80 notched in the 1950s) is a record that will never be broken.

Starting with the 1951 semifinal, the Canadiens and Red Wings met a total of six times in the playoffs during the 1950s. Each team won three times, although all of Detroit's wins came in the finals (1952, 1954, and 1955). Montreal finally took back the Stanley Cup in 1956, gaining revenge for the previous year's defeat without the Rocket. Howe and Richard met head-to-head in 26 playoff games during the 1950s and had remarkably similar statistics during these contests. Richard only holds a slight margin in points (23 to 21), but a larger edge in goals (16 to 9). It is interesting to note that in 1955 Howe had his best finals performance with five goals and seven assists in a seven-game series that was played minus his main rival.

If Richard had an edge in championships over Howe, he could never shake his tormentor entirely. For example, Howe scored his 100th career goal

Most players did their best to avoid Detroit Red Wing Gordie Howe. When he was in a bad mood, Howe could wreak havoc on the opposition physically, or by scoring goals. His 801 career goals remained an NHL record until broken by Wayne Gretzky in 1994.

in Montreal on Maurice Richard Night at the Forum. In 1952-53 Richard fretted as Howe chased his record of 50 goals in a season. His Canadien teammates checked Howe furiously on the last night of the season and kept the Red Wing's total to 49 goals in a 2-1 victory at the Detroit Olympia. Howe never did score 50 goals in a season, and Richard never did win a scoring title (finishing second to Howe twice in 1950-51 and 1953-54), but their on-and-off ice feud continued until the Rocket retired in 1960. In spite of some efforts at reconciliation, the two legends still snipe at each other today.

Such was the nature of the game in the 1950s that bitter enemies remain rivals many years later. The 1950s was the only complete decade in NHL history to feature six teams. The early 1940s still had the New York (later Brooklyn) Americans playing, while the late 1960s witnessed a major expansion that added six new clubs all at once. The 1950s featured some of hockey's greatest moments such as overtime Stanley Cup-winning goals by Pete Babando (Detroit), Bill Barilko (Toronto), Elmer Lach (Montreal), and Tony Leswick (Detroit). The decade also saw the trading of many future Hall of Fame members such as Ted Lindsay, Terry Sawchuk, Bert Olmstead, Bill Gadsby, Allan Stanley, Leo Boivin, Harry Watson, and Harry Lumley.

Keeping one of the 120 NHL jobs in this demanding, defensive era wasn't easy – just ask Johnny Bower or Gump Worsley – and the threat of the minor leagues, which were very good for the most part, hung over every player. With no agents, few players had control of their own destinies, and the owners did whatever pleased them. Anxiety about keeping jobs made for an intense brand of hockey throughout the entire decade. Although there were some attendance problems (mostly in Chicago), the NHL owners had a very stable and profitable business, which they kept on a steady course through to the end of the decade. In 1956 the players finally realized that the NHL was making a great deal of money from their toil. However, any significant player power was still a decade away.

In the pages that follow you will see the photography of Harold Barkley. Like many of the players he captured on film, Barkley set new standards in his field. Born in 1920 in Victoria, British Columbia, Barkley grew up in Toronto and began taking black-and-white hockey photographs for the *Toronto Star* after he graduated from the Ontario College of Art. Best known for his groundbreaking colour action photographs, which will be featured in a second book devoted to the 1960s, the best of the black-and-white Barkley Archives has been chosen for this look at the 1950s, although some colour is included in this volume. Since Barkley was based in Toronto, the majority of photographs are from Maple Leaf Gardens.

Some items that should be noted in these photographs include the thinner rings of the Stanley Cup; the changing uniforms of Boston, Chicago, and the referees; the lack of numbers on the sleeves of the sweaters (early on); how close the fans were to the action (no glass or netting in certain places along the boards); shared penalty boxes; coaches wearing fedoras; clean white boards with no advertising; no helmets or goalie masks (until Jacques Plante in 1959); the overall lack of protection for goalies; and the straight-blade wooden sticks manufactured by CCM and Northland.

The photos are accompanied by captions, anecdotes, and trivia to give some insight into the players and to provide a bit of the era's flavour. And there are special notes on fathers and sons who both played in the NHL. All in all, Harold Barkley captured in photographic amber, as it were, a time in hockey that will never come again. It was, without doubt, the game we knew.

Detroit's Gordie Howe scores on Toronto's Turk Broda while being checked by Howie Meeker. Howe rebounded from a serious injury (he almost died) in the 1950 playoffs to lead the league in goals (43), assists (43, tied with Ted Kennedy), and points (86) in the 1950-51 season. It was the first of six Art Ross Trophies that Howe would win in his career. His first goal in the NHL was scored against Broda and the Leafs on October 16, 1946, in a 3-3 tie. The formidable right winger scored seven times as a rookie and had 22 points. The Calder Trophy went to Meeker, who tallied 27 goals and 45 points as the league's best first-year player in 1946-47. Howe would finish his career with 801 NHL goals, Meeker with 83.

THE MONEY GAME

Gordie Howe was once very unhappy with the Red Wings because they didn't give him the team windbreaker he was promised by Jack Adams. The Detroit manager finally came through and gave Howe the $13.95 jacket as promised. Howie Meeker was even angrier at the Maple Leafs in 1947 because they refused to give him the $1,000 bonus he had in his contract for winning the Calder Trophy. Conn Smythe decided that since the league had paid out $1,000 for winning the award Meeker should be satisfied with that. The future *Hockey Night in Canada* commentator never did get his bonus from the Leafs.

Marketing the Game

During the 1950s, the latest date the Stanley Cup was awarded occurred on April 23, 1950. When the Colorado Avalanche won the Stanley Cup in 1996, they clinched it on June 10.

Gordie Howe

Unusual Note

During the 1950 finals, the New York Rangers couldn't play any home games because the circus took over Madison Square Garden. The circus was the biggest revenue maker for the Garden, and the Rangers had to give up home playoff dates in April. This practice remained in place until 1967 when the Rangers finally got their home playoff games in against Montreal at the Garden.

Marketing the Game

The cost of hockey promotional materials in 1950:

- official NHL record book: $1.00; today $21.95
- subscription to *The Hockey News* (35 issues): $2.50; today $54.95
- 1950 Stanley Cup highlight film: no cost to clubs and organizations; today a video costs $19.95

New York Ranger goalie Chuck Rayner, on the right, poses for a photo with teammate Edgar Laparde. Rayner won only one award in his NHL career, the Hart Trophy as league MVP in 1949-50. He played in 69 games that season, winning 28 times and recording six shutouts. In 1950-51 he won 19 games while playing in 66 contests. His NHL career was over after playing 20 games in 1952-53. A Hall of Famer, Rayner is only one of four Ranger players to win the Hart Trophy (the others are Buddy O'Connor, 1948; Andy Bathgate, 1959; Mark Messier, 1992). Laparde won the Calder Trophy in 1946 and the Lady Byng in 1950. A 10-year Ranger, Laparde played in 500 career games and earned 280 points. He was also elected to the Hall of Fame.

Detroit coach Tommy Ivan shakes the hand of defenceman Leo Reise. Ivan coached the Red Wings to three Stanley Cups in 1950, 1952, and 1954. Prior to joining the Red Wings, he coached in the Detroit farm system at Omaha and Indianapolis before getting the top job in 1947. His regular-season record for the Red Wings was a solid 262-118-90. Ivan left the Wings in 1954 to become general manager of the Chicago Blackhawks and won another Stanley Cup in 1961.

TRIVIA

Leo Reise was a defensive defenceman, but he could rush the puck up the ice when necessary. In the 1950 playoffs Reise scored two overtime-winning goals against the Maple Leafs in a rough seven-game semifinal. His second overtime winner won the series for the Red Wings and ended the three-year reign of the Maple Leafs. Reise finished with only 28 career goals in 494 career games. Teammate Gordie Howe never scored an overtime winner in the playoffs.

TRIVIA

Milt Schmidt was one of many players in the 1950s who later became general managers in the NHL. The list includes Sid Abel, Alex Delvecchio, Emile Francis, Gerry Ehman, Ted Lindsay, Hal Laycoe, Phil Maloney, Max McNab, Bob Pulford, Larry Regan, Red Kelly, and Floyd Smith. Of this group Schmidt was the only one to win a Stanley Cup, while Abel and Francis were the only other ones to get to the finals.

Boston centre Milt Schmidt was the NHL's most valuable player in 1950-51, winning the Hart Trophy for the only time in his career. The Bruins' captain had 22 goals and 39 assists for 61 points in 62 games. In his career, which was played entirely in Boston, Schmidt recorded 229 goals and 575 points in 778 games while winning two Stanley Cups. The Hall of Famer eventually became the coach and general manager of the Bruins between 1963 and 1972, winning two more Stanley Cups. He was also the first general manager of the Washington Capitals in their inaugural 1974-75 season.

Milt Schmidt

Toronto's Max Bentley (*A* on sweater) looks for a loose puck as does his Chicago Blackhawk brother Doug (*C* on sweater). While on a tryout with the Montreal Canadiens, Max Bentley was told by a medical specialist to quit hockey because of a bad heart. But he trained diligently and his brother got him a tryout with Chicago. Max won two Art Ross Trophies with the Blackhawks to go with a Lady Byng Trophy. The Leafs gave up five players to acquire Bentley, and he won three Stanley Cups with Toronto. In 1950-51 Max had 21 goals and 41 assists and added 13 points in 11 playoff games. Doug Bentley had been rejected by Toronto, New York, Boston, and Montreal before he made the Chicago squad in 1939-40. In 1942-43 he won the Art Ross Trophy. Both brothers are in the Hall of Fame.

TRIVIA

In the 1940s and 1950s Chicago made major multiplayer deals to improve a moribund team. When the club traded Max Bentley to Toronto in 1947, he was part of a seven-player deal. On July 13, 1950, the Blackhawks and Red Wings completed a nine-player deal, one of the largest trades in NHL history. Chicago got Metro Prystai, Jim Henry, Bob Goldham, and Gaye Stewart in exchange for Harry Lumley, Al Dewsbury, Don Morrison, Pete Babando, and Jack Stewart. On January 2, 1992, the Toronto Maple Leafs and Calgary Flames completed a 10-player deal, the largest in-season trade in NHL history. The Leafs gave up Gary Leeman, Michel Petit, Alexander Godynyuk, Craig Berube, and Jeff Reese for the Flames' Doug Gilmour, Jamie Macoun, Kent Manderville, Rick Wamsley, and Ric Nattress.

Turk Broda

Toronto goalie Walter "Turk" Broda makes a save against the Boston Bruins on April 8, 1951, in a 6-0 shutout win that sent the Leafs to the finals. The 1951 playoffs marked the last hurrah for the rotund Leaf netminder as he recorded two shutouts and a 1.06 goals-against average in nine playoff games. A clutch performer, Broda won 58 career playoff games while posting a minuscule 1.98 goals-against average with 13 shutouts. The Leafs plucked Broda from the Detroit organization for a cost of $8,000 after a personal scouting trip by Conn Smythe.

TRIVIA

Only three Maple Leafs have been on five Stanley Cup-winning teams: Don Metz (1942, 1945, 1947, 1948, 1949); Ted Kennedy (1945, 1947, 1948, 1949, 1951); and Turk Broda (1942, 1947, 1948, 1949, 1951).

STATSBOX

The 1950-51 Montreal Canadiens became the first team of the decade to make the finals with a losing record (25-30-15). Other teams to make the finals under .500 during the 1950s were Boston (1952-53 and 1957-58) and Toronto (1958-59). None of the four were able to win the Stanley Cup. In more recent years the Minnesota North Stars lost in the finals after finishing 27-39-14 during the 1990-91 season.

A sight not seen in a long time. The Toronto Maple Leafs gather around the Stanley Cup on April 21, 1951, with their coach Joe Primeau (talking to Bill Judza) and backup goalie Turk Broda wearing the suits. Bill Barilko, on the far left, is all smiles after scoring the Cup-winning goal in overtime against Montreal. Barilko was known for his thundering body checks and a willingness to mix it up. He led the league in penalty minutes once (1947-48) and was the inspiration behind four Toronto Stanley Cup wins between 1947 and 1951. Like most defencemen of his era, Barilko was primarily defensive-minded. In 1950-51 he scored six goals and 12 points in the regular season. In the playoffs Barilko scored three goals and had five points in 11 games. Barilko's career totals include 252 games played (all with the Leafs), 26 goals, 36 assists, and 456 penalty minutes.

Unusual Note

The Maple Leafs first called up Bill Barilko from the Hollywood Wolves of the Pacific Coast League in February 1947. The raw but willing rookie was sent to California to learn the professional game. Barilko never played a game for the Leafs' top farm team in Pittsburgh because he earned a roster spot he wouldn't relinquish until his tragic death in a plane crash in the summer of 1951. The defenceman's number 5 was retired by the Leafs.

TRIVIA

A member of the Leafs' legendary Kid Line as a player, Joe Primeau started the 1950-51 season as Toronto's coach. He won the Stanley Cup as a rookie coach after leading the Leafs to a second-place finish with 41 wins and 95 points. With the NHL championship, Primeau became the first coach to win the Stanley Cup, the Memorial Cup (junior hockey), and the Allan Cup (senior hockey). Primeau had turned down the opportunity to coach the Boston Bruins in 1949-50.

The '51 Leafs

TRIVIA

Sid Smith won the Lady Byng Trophy in 1952 and
1955 for the Maple Leafs. Gord Drillon (1938), Syl
Apps (1942), Red Kelly (1961), and Dave Keon
(1962 and 1963) are the only other Leafs to win
the trophy awarded to the most sportsmanlike
player of the season.

Bruin goalie "Sugar" Jim Henry tries to knock the
puck away from Maple Leaf Sid Smith. Boston
purchased Henry from the Detroit Red Wings for
$6,000, and he played his first year as a Bruin in
1951-52. He didn't miss a single regular-season
game for three straight seasons and recorded 22
shutouts during that time. Henry was superb in
the 1953 Bruin semifinal upset of the powerful
Red Wings but was injured in the finals and
missed two games. The 1954-55 season was his last
in the NHL, and he ended his career with a total of
159 wins in 405 games. Smith was a two-time winner of the Lady Byng Trophy (1952 and 1955) who
had his finest playoff performance with the Leafs
in 1951 when he scored seven goals and added
three assists. It marked his third Stanley Cup victory with Toronto.

Detroit's Vic Stasiuk is on his knees and in some trouble against Jim Thomson (A on sweater) and Eric Nesterenko of Toronto. The first NHL player to come from Lethbridge, Alberta, Stasiuk was a solid six foot one and 185 pounds who could hustle and dig the puck out of the corners. He didn't score much as a Red Wing (eight goals in his best year), but he was on two Stanley Cup-winning teams (1952 and 1955). However, a trade to Boston gave Stasiuk a chance to be a goal scorer. From 1956-57 to 1959-60 the left winger had four straight seasons of 20 or more goals. His best NHL season was as a member of the Uke Line in 1959-60 when he had 29 goals and 68 points, finishing ninth in the scoring race. Stasiuk went on to coach three NHL teams – Philadelphia, California, and Vancouver between 1969 and 1973.

THE MONEY GAME

The Maple Leafs thought they had their own version of Jean Beliveau when they scouted Eric Nesterenko. Conn Smythe was so convinced of this that he gave Nesterenko $6,000 to reject a scholarship to the University of Michigan. It wasn't a profitable investment for Toronto since the right winger only played in 206 games in four seasons as a Leaf, scoring 43 times and assisting on another 36. He was dealt to Chicago in May 1956.

Montreal goalie Gerry McNeil gave up two over-time goals that won Stanley Cups. In 1951 the Leafs' Bill Barilko beat him, and in 1954 Tony Leswick put one past him for Detroit. McNeil is the only goalie in NHL history to experience this feeling twice. He won a Stanley Cup with the Canadiens in 1953.

Marketing the Game

Great rivalries between teams was a large part of what attracted fans to the arenas in the six NHL cities of the 1950s. At times a rivalry could over-heat, resulting in wild brawls. This happened on December 9, 1953, when traditional rivals Toronto and Montreal went at it in Maple Leaf Gardens. A bench-clearing brawl featured 15 misconducts, four majors, and 17 minors for a total of 204 penalty minutes, establishing a new NHL record. The current record for most penalty minutes (both teams) in one game occurred in a match between the Boston Bruins and the Minnesota North Stars on February 26, 1981. The warring teams racked up an amazing, if somewhat dismaying, 406 minutes!

Montreal Canadien defenceman Dollard St. Laurent eyes the puck sliding under the shoulder of goalie Gerry McNeil while the Maple Leafs' Fern Flaman hopes for a goal. Montreal teamed St. Laurent with Doug Harvey to form an effective pairing. In seven seasons with the Habs, St. Laurent never scored more than four goals in a season but played his best hockey when he was physical. His last season with Montreal was his best as a Canadien with a career high 20 assists and a total of 23 points. He was then dealt to Chicago to make room for Albert Langlois, who was younger at 24. The 29-year-old St. Laurent moved to the Windy City and played until 1961-62. He won a total of five Stanley Cups (four with Montreal and one with Chicago) before he retired.

THE MONEY GAME

Marty Pavelich started a business with teammate Ted Lindsay while they were still playing in the NHL. Not surprisingly in the Motor City, they began selling automobile parts and then switched to the manufacturing end of the business. It provided them with a good income, and postcareer success was assured, but Detroit manager Jack Adams wasn't pleased. Adams practically forced Gordie Howe out of a partnership with Lindsay and Pavelich, and he later traded Lindsay. Pavelich was forced to retire at the age of 29 to run the business when Adams insisted the players devote themselves solely to hockey.

Three members of the Red Wings, (*left to right*) Ted Lindsay, Sid Abel, and Marty Pavelich, enjoy a postgame 7-Up. Pavelich played a primary checking role on the four Detroit Stanley Cup teams of the 1950s. He was often teamed with Glen Skov and Tony Leswick. Pavelich's best year was 1951-52 when he scored 17 goals and achieved 36 points. In 10 seasons with the Wings, Pavelich only had 93 goals but did manage 159 assists in 634 career games. Abel played for 12 years in Detroit, winning three Cups before going to Chicago in 1952-53. The Red Wing captain finished with 472 career points in 613 games.

The Chicago Blackhawks' right winger Bill Mosienko (8) whacks at a loose puck against Maple Leaf goalie Al Rollins. A native of Winnipeg, Mosienko began his career in the mid-1940s and had 32 goals in 50 games in 1943-44, his first full season with Chicago. He had three seasons of 20 or more goals before breaking the 30-goal barrier again in 1951-52. He finished with 31 that year; his final three goals were scored in 21 seconds (an NHL record yet to be broken) against the New York Rangers. A onetime Lady Byng Trophy winner in 1945, Mosienko finished his Hall of Fame career with 258 goals and 540 points in 710 games.

TRIVIA

Chicago centre Gus Bodnar assisted on all three of Bill Mosienko's record-setting goals. The only other player to assist Mosienko in his 21-second blitz was Blackhawk forward George Gee.

Unusual Note

Lorne Anderson was in net on March 23, 1952, when Bill Mosienko set his record. Anderson played in only three games in 1951-52 for the Rangers, winning one and losing two. He never played in the NHL again, much like Dave Reece of Boston, who allowed a still-unbroken record of 10 points by Darryl Sittler in one game. Reece played in 14 games in 1975-76 with a 7-5-2 record and two shutouts.

STATSBOX

By 1952-53 Rocket Richard had scored 344 goals and Elmer Lach had assisted on 150 of them. Lach's last NHL season was 1953-54 when he played in 48 games.

Unusual Note

In 1955 longtime NHL referee Red Storey listed items that had been thrown at him by fans in the six big-league cities: apples, hats, rubber overshoes, peanuts, coins, programs, a live baby octopus, and a five-pound bag of split peas.

Montreal's Elmer Lach and Toronto's Ted Kennedy make their arguments to referee Red Storey. Lach played an aggressive game as a Canadien centre for 14 seasons and was named a first-team all-star three times in his career. During the 1940s, he won the Hart Trophy (1945) and the Art Ross Trophy twice (1945 and 1948). Lach scored two goals against Boston on the last night of the 1947-48 season to edge out the Rangers' Buddy O'Connor 61 points to 60 for the Art Ross. At one point Lach held the following NHL records: most assists in one season, 54 (1944-45); most career assists, 408; and most career points, 548. He scored the Cup-winning goal in overtime against Boston in 1953.

Elmer
Lach

Radio and television broadcasting legend Foster Hewitt makes the long trek up to the gondola, 54 feet above centre ice at Maple Leaf Gardens. Hewitt's "Hello Canada and hockey fans in Canada and the United States" was heard only on radio until Saturday, November 1, 1952. On that night *Hockey Night in Canada* made its debut on television, joining the game in progress at 9:30 p.m., and Hewitt did a simulcast on both radio and television. Toronto beat Boston 3-2. The games were broadcast in this fashion for a while, but eventually Hewitt returned to radio and let his son Bill handle the television duties. Today *Hockey Night in Canada* pulls in an average of 1.2 million viewers during the season and millions more for the Stanley Cup playoffs, depending on the teams involved. The games now start at 7:30 p.m. and two contests are shown each Saturday.

THE MONEY GAME

Toronto owner Conn Smythe sold the television rights for 1952-53 for $100 a game mostly because he wasn't sure how the game would go over on television. Once the experiment was deemed a success, Smythe then asked for $150,000 for the season. By the early 1960s Conn's son Stafford sold the rights to the Leaf television broadcasts for $21,000 a game.

Unusual Note

Butch Bouchard is one of four former Canadien captains who opened up a bar/restaurant in Montreal at some point in their lives. The others are Toe Blake, Henri Richard, and Yvan Cournoyer.

TRIVIA

At the beginning of the 1956-57 season Harry Watson was one of only four active players to have scored 200 or more goals in their careers. The others were Rocket Richard, Gordie Howe, and Ted Lindsay.

Montreal Canadien captain Emile "Butch" Bouchard keeps an eye on the Maple Leafs' Harry Watson while goalie Gerry McNeil looks for the puck. Bouchard took on veteran Murph Chamberlain in his second training camp and, in winning the battle, he impressed his teammates and coach Dick Irvin. The big defenceman didn't learn to skate until he was 16 and played only 80 games as an amateur. Bouchard learned to use his size (six foot two, 205 pounds) and how to position himself on the ice for 15 NHL seasons with the Canadiens. He played on four Stanley Cup teams for the Habs. Bouchard's son Pierre also played for the Canadiens and won five Cups during the 1970s.

Butch
Bouchard

STATSBOX

The NHL record for the fewest goals against in a minimum 70-game season is held by the Toronto Maple Leafs of 1953-54 when goalies Harry Lumley and Gil Mayer allowed only 131 goals. The Montreal Canadiens equalled this mark in 1955-56 when they were backstopped by Jacques Plante and Bobby Perreault. The next best record is held by the 1953-54 Red Wings with 132, while the Detroit teams of 1951-52 and 1952-53 allowed 133 goals. In 1973-74 both the Chicago Blackhawks and the Philadelphia Flyers were only scored on 164 times in a 78-game schedule, while in 1976-77 the Montreal Canadiens allowed just 171 goals in an 80-game schedule.

Toronto goalie Harry Lumley is surrounded by Boston players Joe Klukay, Ed Sandford (A on sweater), and Warren Godfrey (6). Lumley started his NHL career as a 17-year-old in 1943-44 when he played two games for Detroit. After six seasons as a Red Wing, including a Cup win in 1950, he was traded to Chicago to make room for Terry Sawchuk. In 1952 he was sent to Toronto and led the league with 10 shutouts. The 1953-54 season saw Lumley win the Vezina Trophy with a 1.85 goals-against average and 13 shutouts. In 1954-55 Lumley lost the Vezina on the last night of the regular schedule when he let in six goals, allowing Terry Sawchuk to win the trophy by one goal. Lumley finished his career with the Boston Bruins and earned a total of 71 shutouts.

Boston centre Dave Creighton battles Toronto defenceman Fern Flaman to get a shot at Harry Lumley. Creighton was a top prospect in the late 1940s as a member of the Port Arthur (Ontario) Bruins when they won the Memorial Cup. He turned professional with Boston and scored a goal against Chuck Rayner of the Rangers on his first shot in the NHL. Creighton had the first of three 20-goal seasons in the league during 1951-52 with Boston, but his best years were in New York playing between Camille Henry and Andy Hebenton. By the age of 25 Creighton had played for the Bruins, Rangers, Maple Leafs, and Blackhawks. He managed a respectable 314 points in 616 career games.

Fathers and Sons

Dave Creighton's son Adam was a high draft choice of the Buffalo Sabres (11th overall in 1983) after a great junior career with Ottawa in the Ontario Hockey Association (OHA). He has played for five NHL teams (as of 1996-97), and his best year was in Chicago when he had 34 goals and 70 points. To date he has 403 points in 708 career games.

Marketing the Game

During the 1950s, players on the U.S.-based teams used sticks made by Northland, a company based in St. Paul, Minnesota. The firm's advertising boasted that these sticks made "more goals than any other" and that they were "made especially for bruising play."

THE MONEY GAME

The NHL had no reservations about playing games on Christmas Eve or Christmas Day during the 1950s. For example, in 1955-56 the schedule lists two games for December 24 – Detroit at Montreal and Chicago at Toronto. The lineup for December 25 shows three games – Chicago at Boston, Toronto at Detroit, and Montreal at New York. The Rangers had a tradition of playing at home on Christmas night and enjoyed a great record for games played on December 25. In fact, when they lost on Christmas 1957, it was their first defeat on that night in 29 years.

The New York Rangers' Wally Hergesheimer takes a shot on Maple Leaf goalie Harry Lumley. A slow, small player who lacked a great shot, Hergesheimer was excellent at scoring goals by hanging around the crease. After three years in the minors, he made the Rangers in 1951-52 and scored 26 goals. He followed that up with seasons of 30 and 27 goals. In 1954 he suffered a broken leg and, fearing for his job, came back too soon. As a result, he broke the leg a second time. However, in 1955-56, his first full season back, he scored 22 times. Hergesheimer was dealt to Chicago for Red Sullivan but returned to the Rangers for 22 games in 1958-59. His final record shows 114 goals in 351 games, and he was the second player in history to score 100 goals in both the NHL and AHL.

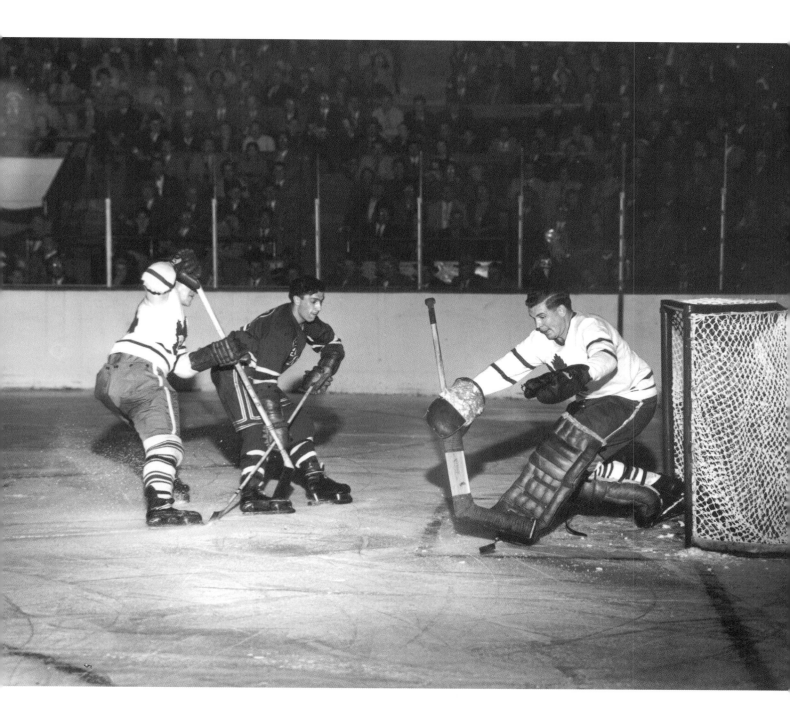

Chicago goalie Al Rollins stops Toronto's Tim Horton (7). Rollins tried to start his NHL career with the New York Rangers, but the team rejected him because of his rheumatic heart. Refusing to quit the game, Rollins finally made it to the NHL with Toronto in 1950-51. He won the Vezina Trophy that year and led the league in wins with 27. Rollins was in the Leaf net when Bill Barilko scored his famous overtime goal to win the Stanley Cup. The Leafs dealt Rollins to Chicago in September 1952, and in 1953-54 he was named the winner of the Hart Trophy as MVP. That season he only won 12 times, although he did record five shutouts. It was his second great season with a poor Blackhawk team (he had finished second to Gordie Howe in the Hart Trophy race in 1952-53), and his performance was recognized by the voters.

TRIVIA

When Al Rollins won the Hart Trophy in 1953-54, he was the first Blackhawk to win the award since 1945-46 when Max Bentley became the first Chicago player to earn it. The only other Chicago Hart Trophy winners were Bobby Hull and Stan Mikita, who both won it twice in the 1960s.

Al Rollins

THE MONEY GAME

Johnny Bower disliked the uncertainties of playing in the NHL, so when the Maple Leafs came to
sign him in 1958, he asked for a two-year deal
with moving expenses, no demotions to the
minors, and a guarantee that he would be paid in
full if injured even if the injury occurred in training camp. Bower was used to such negotiations
because he had a clause in his final minor-league
contract that stipulated he couldn't be sold or
traded without his approval. He was unable to
stop the Leafs from drafting him, but his
demands must have been looked after because,
in the end, he did sign with Toronto.

New York goalie Johnny Bower slides out to stop
Toronto's Bob Solinger, with Ron Murphy (*left*)
and Allan Stanley (*right*) trying to gather up a
rebound. Bower had played eight years in the
American Hockey League, where he was named
the best goalie twice, before he got a chance in the
NHL with the Rangers in 1953-54. He played in all
70 games and recorded five shutouts and a 2.60
goals-against average. The next season he returned
to the minors and stayed there until 1958 when
Toronto picked him up in the intraleague draft.
Bower proved he belonged in the NHL by taking
the Maple Leafs to the finals in 1959 and 1960.

TRIVIA

All-star games usually feature lots of goals, especially in recent years, but on October 23, 1956,
Johnny Bower stopped all 47 shots taken by the
AHL All-Stars against the Providence Reds. Providence won 4-0 in what became the only professional all-star game ever to feature a shutout.

Johnny Bower

Harry Watson played in the NHL as a 19-year-old in 1941-42 with the New York Americans. Watson was the last New York American player to retire when he left the NHL after the 1957-58 season. One of the top "power forwards" of this era, Watson was a good skater who had a powerful shot. A durable and consistent performer, Watson was respected by the opposition for his toughness and goal-scoring abilities. He scored 236 career goals and was elected to the Hall of Fame.

The Montreal Canadiens' Bert Olmstead tries to lift the puck over the Leafs' Harry Lumley while Harry Watson attempts to check the big left winger. In December 1950 the Canadiens acquired Olmstead in a trade with Detroit by giving up Leo Gravelle. The trade turned out to be a steal for the Canadiens, who added a tough, hard-nosed winger able to dig pucks out of the corners and make pin-point passes. In fact, Olmstead once held the NHL record for most assists in a season when he tallied 56 helpers in 1955-56. He also led the NHL in assists in 1954-55 with 48. Further proof of his playmaking prowess is the record for most points in a game (four goals and four assists) that he set in a 12-1 slaughter of Chicago on January 9, 1954. That achievement tied a mark established by Rocket Richard and wasn't surpassed until Toronto's Darryl Sittler nailed 10 points in a game against Boston on February 7, 1976.

New York Ranger left winger Nick Mickoski (11) tries to track a high-flying puck but must contend with Maple Leaf defencemen Leo Boivin (*left*) and Jim Morrison (*right*). Mickoski was nearly a hero for the Rangers in the 1950 finals against Detroit. He hit the post with a shot in overtime just before the Red Wings' Pete Babando scored to win the Stanley Cup for Detroit. The Ranger scored 20 goals in 1950-51 and had 19 markers three other times. He played in 703 games in his NHL career, which included stops in Chicago, Detroit, and Boston, and scored a total of 158 goals and 185 assists.

Unusual Note

Nick Mickoski was scouted in his native Winnipeg by the New York Rangers. He was one of many future NHL players who played for the Winnipeg Excelsiors, a bantam-age hockey club. Jim Thomson, Don Raleigh, Andy Bathgate, Wally Hergesheimer, and Bill Ezinicki all played for the Excelsiors and toiled in the NHL during the 1950s. All of these players were also born in Winnipeg. Other natives of Winnipeg who played in the NHL during this decade were Bill Mosienko, Terry Sawchuk, Andy Hebenton, Eddie Mazur, and Ab McDonald. The total number of NHL players in 1996-97 who were born in Winnipeg was seven.

Unusual Note

As a Junior B hockey player, Earl Reibel was in a car with five teammates when it stalled on railway tracks in Kitchener, his hometown. An oncoming train hit the car, but no player was killed and Reibel suffered only fractured ribs. He went on to have a six-year career in the NHL, playing in 409 games and recording 245 points (84 goals and 161 assists). A much more deadly accident occurred on December 30, 1986, when four players of the Junior A Swift Current (Saskatchewan) Broncos were killed in a tragic team bus crash. Future Colorado Avalanche star Joe Sakic was one of the survivors.

The Red Wings' Earl Reibel circles the net with the puck to start a rush up the ice. A playmaking centre with a hard pass and accurate shot, Reibel's first NHL game was quite memorable. On October 8, 1953, Reibel set an NHL record for most assists by a rookie in his first game. Reibel's four assists came against the New York Rangers in a 4-1 victory. The record still hasn't been broken and was only tied once by Roland Erikson of the Minnesota North Stars on October 6, 1976. Reibel scored 15 goals as a rookie and finished with 33 assists. He had a better year in 1954-55 when he notched 25 goals and had 66 points (good for fourth overall in league scoring). Reibel topped off a great year with 12 points in the playoffs as Detroit won the Stanley Cup. He was awarded the Lady Byng Trophy the next season, but his play declined after that year. In 1957-58 he was traded to Chicago.

Detroit's Bill Dineen, far left, hustles to bat the puck out of midair and into the Toronto net. Red Wing Ted Lindsay also eyes the puck as do, left to right, Tod Sloan, Tim Horton, and Harry Lumley of the Leafs. As a rookie in 1953-54, Dineen scored 17 goals for the Stanley Cup champion Red Wings and was promptly offered a $500 raise by manager Jack Adams, giving him a yearly salary of $6,500.

What Adams neglected to tell Dineen was that $6,500 had become the NHL's minimum salary. The right winger stayed in Detroit until 1957 when he was shipped off to Chicago. The 1957-58 season was his last as a player, but he returned to the NHL as coach of the Philadelphia Flyers between 1991 and 1993. Coaching players such as his son Kevin and new superstar Eric Lindros, Dineen tallied a coaching record of 60-60-20.

Fathers and Sons

Bill Dineen has had three sons play in the NHL. The NHL statistics for the Dineen family at the end of the 1996-97 season were as follows: Bill (323 games, 51 goals, 44 assists); Peter (13 games, 0 goals, 2 assists); Gord (528 games, 16 goals, 90 assists); and Kevin (871 games, 323 goals, 356 assists). Gord and Kevin are still active in professional hockey.

Montreal's Rocket Richard (*A* on sweater) is checked by Toronto's Leo Boivin, Tod Sloan, and Jim Morrison. Goalie Harry Lumley looks worried. The Canadiens nearly gave up on Richard when he was injured so often early in his career. But by the time he retired, Richard was a sports legend and almost a deity in his native Quebec. His legendary reputation was largely built in the playoffs when he played his best hockey. An eight-time Stanley Cup winner, Richard still holds the NHL record of six overtime-winning goals in the playoffs (Glenn Anderson is next with five), and his 18 game winners are second only to Wayne Gretzky's 24. His last great playoff performance came in the 1957 finals against Boston when he whipped four goals past Don Simmons in the first game. When the Montreal Forum closed in 1996, it was the Rocket who got the longest and loudest ovation.

TRIVIA

Maurice Richard was the first NHL player to record 500 career goals. When he scored the 500th goal on October 19, 1957, against Glenn Hall of Chicago, Richard, at 36, was the oldest player in the NHL.

Marketing the Game

During the mid-1950s, the Chicago Blackhawks played some "home" games in other U.S. cities. One such contest was held in St. Louis against the Canadiens. In a pregame ceremony Rocket Richard presented his famous sweater number 9 to baseball player Stan Musial. In 1979 the Rocket's sweater was immortalized in Quebec author Roch Carrier's children's story, "The Hockey Sweater."

TRIVIA

The 1956-57 Chicago Blackhawks training camp featured three sets of brothers competing for NHL jobs. Johnny and Larry Wilson, Fred and Sandy Hucul, and Pierre and Florent Pilote battled for places on the struggling Blackhawks. Johnny Wilson and Pierre Pilote were the only two to stay with Chicago that season.

Unusual Note

Johnny Wilson coached four different NHL teams between 1969 and 1980. In 1976-77, when he coached the Colorado Rockies, his brother Larry was also coaching in the NHL with the Red Wings. The Patrick brothers, Lynn (Boston) and Muzz (New York), also coached in the NHL at the same time between 1953 and 1955. Between 1990 and 1993 the Murray brothers, Bryan (Detroit) and Terry (Washington), also shared the same experience. Larry Wilson's son Ron was named the first coach of the Anaheim Mighty Ducks in 1993.

Detroit's Johnny Wilson, far left, keeps an eye on his man, while the Leafs' Bob Bailey takes a shot on goalie Terry Sawchuk. Wilson once held the NHL's ironman mark when he played in 580 consecutive games for the Red Wings, Blackhawks, and Maple Leafs between 1952 and 1960. Wilson was first noticed when he attended a prospects camp for Detroit players in September 1947. He did well in the minors (80 points one year at Omaha) before joining the Wings in 1951-52. The hardworking left winger scored 23 goals in 1952-53 and was a Red Wing for four Stanley Cup wins (1950, 1952, 1954, 1955). Detroit dealt him to Chicago in 1955.

Johnny Wilson

Toronto's George Armstrong (10) and Harry Watson (*A* on sweater) try to get a handle on a loose puck against Detroit's Terry Sawchuk in goal and Bob Goldham on defence. Armstrong scored his first goal in the NHL against Montreal on February 9, 1952. He took a pass from Max Bentley, got around Canadien defenceman Butch Bouchard, and beat goalie Gerry McNeil for the winning goal in a 3-2 victory. For the most part, Armstrong was a poor, plodding skater who had an unspectacular shot in his early years with Toronto. He improved steadily, and by 1958-59 he hit the coveted 20-goal mark. By that time he had been named Leaf captain and followed up with 23 goals in 1959-60. At the close of the decade Armstrong was known as a solid two-way player. He was the last Leaf captain named by Conn Smythe.

TRIVIA

George Armstrong was given sweater number 10 by Toronto manager Conn Smythe, who had previously said no one would get that number after Syl Apps retired. The Maple Leafs who have worn this number since Armstrong's retirement in 1970-71 include George Ferguson, John Anderson, Vince Damphousse, Bill Berg, and Zdenek Nedved.

Unusual Note

Special nights to honour players are usually reserved for stars. However, the Red Wings held a tribute to Bob Goldham on March 3, 1955. Goldham excelled at the defensive aspects of the game and was great at blocking shots. He was so good at it that he became known as the "assistant goalie." One of Goldham's gifts was a station wagon that was purchased in Windsor, Ontario (for duty-tax reasons). The only other Wings honoured up to that point were Syd Howe and Sid Abel.

STATSBOX

Ted Kennedy still holds the Maple Leaf record for most points in the Stanley Cup finals with 23. George Armstrong and Frank Mahovlich are next with 22 each, followed by Syl Apps and Bob Pulford with 21 each.

THE MONEY GAME

The Maple Leafs talked Ted Kennedy into coming out of retirement to help the team during 1956-57 but initially refused to pay him the salary he earned the previous year. Kennedy stood firm and got what he wanted for the last 30 games of the season. He contributed six goals and 16 assists, but the Leafs missed the playoffs.

Maple Leaf captain Ted Kennedy gets a pass away before the Red Wings' Tony Leswick can check him. Leaf owner and manager Conn Smythe often called "Teeder" Kennedy the greatest Leaf of all time, and few would argue. Kennedy showed leadership, discipline, and a hate-to-lose attitude that endeared him to Smythe and all Leaf fans. He wasn't a great skater, but he was a relentless forechecker who excelled at face-offs. Like his idol, former Leaf star Charlie Conacher, Teeder wore sweater number 9, and his mentor was Nels Stewart, who coached him as a youngster. Stewart, a great goal scorer in his day, told Kennedy to "look before you shoot and don't rush." The Leaf star learned his lessons well, scoring 231 career goals for Toronto and winning the Hart Trophy in 1955. In 696 career games Kennedy also added 329 assists for 560 total points. Like Kennedy, "Tough Tony" Leswick scored a Stanley Cup winning-goal when a fluke shot ended a seventh-game overtime battle with Montreal in 1954.

STATSBOX

Bill Quackenbush, a five-time all-star performer as a defenceman, once played in 131 consecutive games without taking a penalty. He took a tripping penalty on January 26, 1950, to break the streak. While he was with Detroit, he won the Lady Byng Trophy in 1948-49, becoming the first defenceman to do so. Quackenbush played in 774 career games and only recorded 95 penalty minutes. A classic defensive defenceman, Quackenbush did manage 62 goals and 222 assists in his career, which ended after the 1955-56 season.

Boston defenceman Hal Laycoe, wearing glasses, tries to take the puck from Toronto's Ron Stewart after goalie "Sugar" Jim Henry has kicked it out. Bill Quackenbush is the other defenceman just behind Laycoe; the other Leaf forward is Sid Smith. It is ironic that the not overly aggressive Laycoe started the events that eventually led to the Richard Riot on March 17, 1955. The Bruin cut Richard with his stick, and the Rocket went ballistic trying to get at Laycoe. During the donneybrook, Richard punched a linesman, earning a suspension with vast repercussions. The Montreal fans' reaction to losing a legend for the playoffs was to take to the streets and do considerable damage. Laycoe had been a onetime teammate of Richard's, but the Canadiens had dealt him to Boston where he played until 1955-56. Laycoe appeared in a total of 531 career games (he had started with New York) and scored 25 goals and 102 points while recording 292 penalty minutes.

Boston's Leo Labine raises his stick high against Eric Nesterenko of Toronto. Labine joined the Bruins full-time in 1952-53 when he played in 51 games and scored eight goals. Known as a gadfly on the ice, he was also a tough body checker with a deft touch around the net. He scored a career best of 24 goals in 1954-55 and had a high mark of 47 points two years later, but he became best known for tying an NHL record with five points in one period (three goals, two assists) on November 28, 1954, in a 6-2 win over Detroit. Labine tied a record held at the time by Les Cunningham and Max Bentley. Seven other players also achieved this feat, starting in 1976 with Darryl Sittler. Bryan Trottier broke the mark with six points (three goals, three assists) in a 1978 game between New York's Islanders and Rangers.

Marketing the Game

The 1950s featured many great nicknames for players who became readily identifiable by their monikers. Leo Labine's "Haileybury Comet," derived from his hometown of Haileybury, Ontario, and his skating style, was one of the best. Other great nicknames of the decade include "Terrible" Ted Lindsay, "Bashing" Bill Barilko, Max "Dipsy Doodle Dandy" Bentley, Bert "Dirtie Bertie" Olmstead, and Bernie "Boom Boom" Geoffrion.

A common sight during the 1950s was two players sharing a seat in the penalty box. Here Boston's Leo Boivin (20) and Toronto's Bob Bailey (18) sit cozily together. Sometimes an usher or policeman would sit between the two combatants, although that isn't the case here, which is surprising since both players were well-known tough guys. Boivin began his long career as an NHL defenceman for the Leafs in 1951. A terrific body checker, Boivin was supposed to replace Bill Barilko. He recorded 97 penalty minutes for the Leafs in 1952-53 but was dealt to Boston in November 1954 where he became a consistent performer for many years. Bailey was essentially a minor-league right winger, but he played in parts of three seasons with the Leafs. He also played for Detroit and Chicago, totalling 150 NHL games, 15 goals, and 207 penalty minutes. He was best known for a run-in with Rocket Richard, whose retaliation was severe and decisive.

Marketing the Game

The St. Lawrence Starch Company of Port Credit, Ontario, produced five-by-seven black-and-white photographs of NHL players each season during the 1950s (the company actually started doing this in 1934). Lists of players from all six teams were provided to fans so they could select their favourites. All that was required was one label (per photograph), showing proof of purchase of company products such as corn syrup, corn starch, or laundry starch. Since most of the labels came from Beehive Corn Syrup, the photographs became known as "Beehives."

Unusual Note

Real Chevrefils was one of many players to play minor-league hockey in Hershey, Pennsylvania, during the 1950s and then play in the NHL. The Hershey arena was built in 1936 and had a capacity of 7,200. In 1957-58 the Hockey Bears drew a total of 189,000 fans, which is quite remarkable considering the population of the town at the time was only 4,500. Hershey is still the home of the famous chocolate company, and the Bears are now affiliated with the Colorado Avalanche.

The Boston Bruins' Real Chevrefils, far left, takes a shot at Maple Leaf goalie Harry Lumley while Gord Hannigan prepares to defend against a rebound. After helping the Barrie Flyers win the Memorial Cup in 1951, Chevrefils joined the Bruins during the 1951-52 season. He quickly impressed management and fans with 25 points in 33 games. Known as a finesse player, he suffered a broken leg in 1953-54 and played in only 14 games that season. He bounced back to score 18 times in 1954-55 but was dealt to the Red Wings to start the next year. He never quite fit in with Detroit and was promptly traded back to the Bruins. In 1956-57 Chevrefils scored 31 goals to become the first Bruin to get more than 30 since Bobby Bauer in 1946-47. His last NHL season was 1958-59, and he finished with 104 career goals in 387 games.

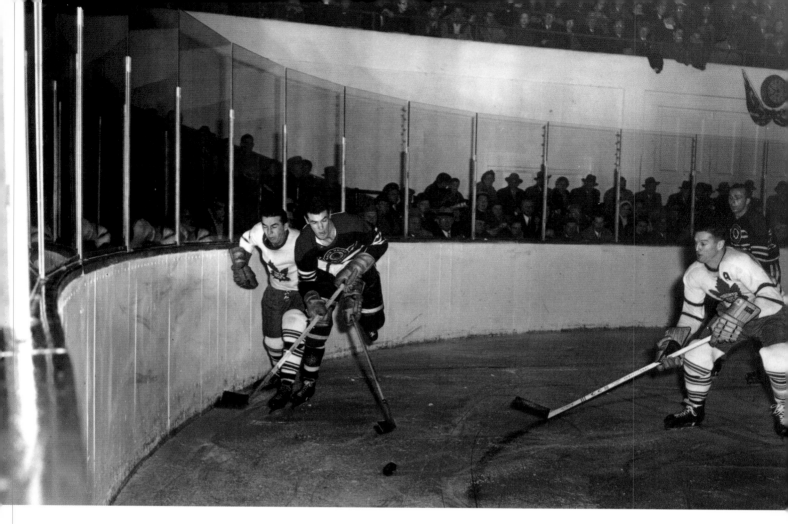

Chicago's Eddie Litzenberger takes out Toronto's Ron Stewart against the boards. Litzenberger began his rookie year, 1954-55, with the Montreal Canadiens, but when the NHL developed a Save the Blackhawks plan to help out the floundering club, the Canadiens gave him up, electing to keep veteran Floyd Curry instead. Litzenberger ended up playing in 73 games (the regular schedule called for 70) and finished with 23 goals and 51 points to win the Calder Trophy as best rookie. Tall and somewhat awkward, Litzenberger kept improving and had three straight seasons of 30 or more goals, which earned him a second-team all-star selection in 1957. He was named captain of Chicago in 1958 and helped the Blackhawks win the Stanley Cup in 1961; the team hasn't won a Cup since.

Unusual Note

Toronto's Ron Stewart once took a Doug Harvey elbow that broke his jaw. A man named Doug Laurie, a sporting goods expert with a store in Maple Leaf Gardens, designed a face mask that covered the jaw area, although most of the face was still exposed. It offered enough protection to allow Stewart to play with his jaw wired.

Unusual Note

Like all great coaches, Dick Irvin had a sharp eye for detail. While he was coaching the Montreal Canadiens he noticed that Toronto goalie Harry Lumley was using an illegal stick. A measurement revealed that Lumley's stick blade was four inches wide instead of the regulation three inches. Lumley was furious, but the coach made his point.

Montreal coach Dick Irvin directs his team from behind the bench. Irvin began his coaching career with Chicago and made the finals with the Blackhawks but lost to the Montreal Canadiens. He then moved to Toronto and took the Maple Leafs to the finals seven times, winning once in 1932. After joining the Canadiens, Irvin took that club to the finals a total of eight times, capturing the Stanley Cup on three occasions (1944, 1946, 1953). In all, Irvin made it to the finals a remarkable 16 times (the next closest is coach Scotty Bowman with 11). He also holds the record for most wins in the finals with 32. Irvin's overall playoff record is 100 wins, 88 defeats, and four Stanley Cups.

Dick Irvin

Detroit goalie Terry Sawchuk comes out to stop Toronto's Tim Horton (7) while teammate Benny Woit holds on to Tod Sloan. A Chicago scout tried to sign Sawchuk for the Blackhawks, but the goaltender's father said no. A day later, though, Detroit scout Bob Kinnear visited the Sawchuk home in Winnipeg, and this time the answer was yes. In his first five years with the Red Wings, Sawchuk won the Vezina Trophy three times while recording 56 shutouts, and his goals-against average never rose above 2.00. In addition, he won the Calder Trophy (1950-51) and was an all-star five times. In spite of this outstanding performance he was dealt to Boston in 1955.

STATSBOX

In the 1952 playoffs Terry Sawchuk recorded four shutouts (two against Toronto and two against Montreal), tying an NHL record for most shutouts in one playoff year. The record has since been tied by only four other goalies: Bernie Parent (1975), Ken Dryden (1977), Mike Richter (1994), and Kirk McLean (1994).

Unusual Note

By the age of 30 Terry Sawchuk had had 66 bone chips removed from his elbow and several broken teeth extracted from his jawbone. He had also undergone an emergency appendectomy, suffered a severe chest injury from an auto accident, and contracted mononucleosis (while with the Boston Bruins).

Terry
Sawchuk

THE MONEY GAME

Ted Lindsay's battles weren't limited to those on the ice. He began a war with management when he realized just how lucrative a business the NHL was even during the 1950s. Although he was hated by players such as Doug Harvey (Montreal), Fern Flaman (Boston), Jim Thomson (Toronto), Bill Gadsby (New York), and Gus Mortson (Chicago), Lindsay approached them with the idea of forming a players' association. The man the least likely to head a union of players got everyone to put $100 toward the association. On February 12, 1957, the short-lived "union" was announced and Lindsay was forever despised by NHL management, especially by his own boss, Jack Adams. Association organizers such as Lindsay and Thomson and perceived sympathizers such as Jack Evans and Tod Sloan were all traded to the Chicago Blackhawks, the league doormat.

Detroit's Ted Lindsay (7) is his usual combative self while exchanging a few choice words with the officials during a game at Maple Leaf Gardens. Bob Goldham (*A* on sweater) is the other Red Wing. Lindsay played junior hockey for St. Michael's in Toronto, but the Maple Leafs' scout missed out on the smallish winger (five foot eight, 160 pounds) when he saw a game that Lindsay didn't appear in because of an injury. Detroit scout Carson Cooper did see Lindsay play and quickly signed him up for the Red Wings. Wanting to prove that he belonged, the pugnacious Lindsay never let anybody intimidate him. This attitude made Terrible Ted's stick and fists feared items, although he had many challengers. He once admitted to having 250 stitches in his face as a result of his many battles. But Lindsay could also score (379 career goals) and play the game (eight-time all-star). When he retired after the 1964-65 season, Lindsay was considered the best left winger in NHL history.

Boston's Johnny Peirson (*A* on sweater) waits in front of the net for a pass while the Maple Leafs' George Armstrong is poised to move in and intercept. A native of Winnipeg, Peirson scored 20 or more goals four times in his career. His best mark in goals was 27 in 1949-50, and he had a career high of 52 points that season. Although he was known for his scoring, Peirson was also a good defensive player who wasn't afraid to backcheck. At the age of 29 he decided to retire and pursue business opportunities at the end of the 1953-54 season. After one year away, he came back to play in 1955-56 and helped Boston to the finals twice. He then retired for good in 1958, finishing with 153 career goals in 545 games.

STATSBOX

During the 1950s, a player who scored 20 or more goals was considered to have had a very good if not excellent season. Any goal scorer who could produce 20 goals consistently was very valuable to his team. In 1954-55 only 13 players scored 20 or more goals, making such producers a rarity. In 1995-96 a total of 117 players had at least 20 goals.

Johnny Peirson

Marketing the Game

One of the first monthly hockey magazines was *Blueline*, published out of Montreal. In 1955 it sold for 25 cents, and in addition to stories of NHL players, the magazine also had articles on the minor leagues. Each issue featured an advertisement that offered readers eight-by-eleven glossy photographs of their favourite stars. Suitable for framing, each photo cost 25 cents, or five could be bought for $1.

Unusual Note

Fleming Mackell was a devout, churchgoing Roman Catholic who fathered six children while he was in the NHL. Mackell said this gave him all the motivation he needed to play as well as he could every game.

The Boston Bruins' Fleming Mackell (8) reaches for a loose puck against Leaf defenceman Jim Morrison at the side of the goal. Originally a Maple Leaf who played a major role in Toronto's 1949 and 1951 Stanley Cup wins, Mackell became a solid goal scorer as a Bruin between 1952 and 1960. One of the league's fastest skaters, Mackell scored a career high 27 goals in 1952-53 for Boston and added nine points in 11 playoff games. Mackell helped Boston to the finals again in 1957 and 1958 when he set a playoff record with 14 assists in 12 games. Wayne Gretzky, while playing for the Edmonton Oilers, amassed a record 31 assists in 19 games in the 1988 playoffs. The 1957-58 season saw Mackell score 20 times and earn a career-best 60 points. He finished his career with 369 points in 665 games. Mackell was named to the first-team all-stars once (1952-53).

Fleming
Mackell

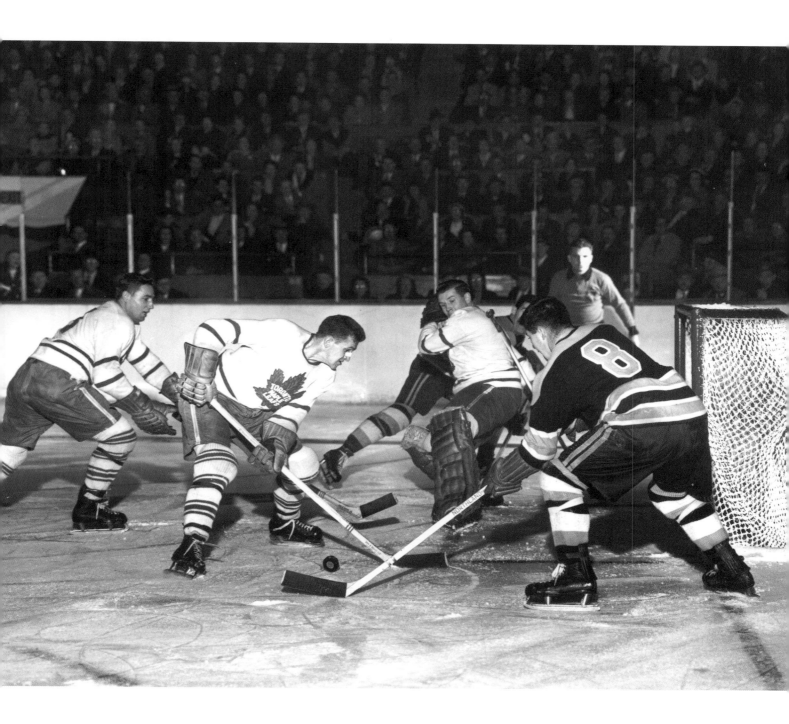

THE MONEY GAME

Early in his career Bernie Geoffrion signed a contract that gave him a $1,000 bonus for scoring 20 goals. For every goal after 20 he got another $100. In 1996-97 the Toronto Maple Leafs gave player Tie Domi a contract with a clause that would earn him $50,000 for 10 goals or 25 points, provided the Leafs made the playoffs.

Fathers and Sons

Like his famous father, Bernie, Danny Geoffrion played for the Montreal Canadiens. Danny only played in 32 games for the Habs in 1979-80 when his father coached the team for part of the season. He didn't get a goal and had just six assists. However, in 1980-81, Danny moved to the Winnipeg Jets and tallied 20 goals in 78 games.

Bernie "Boom Boom" Geoffrion (5) of the Canadiens tries to lift the puck over a fallen Harry Lumley. The nickname was given to Geoffrion by sportswriter Charlie Boire, who suggested "Boom" after hearing the sound of Geoffrion's shot after it hit the boards. It was Geoffrion who added the second "Boom." In 1951-52 Geoffrion fired in 30 goals to help him win the Calder Trophy. His slap shot terrorized goalies from then on. In 1954-55 he won his first Art Ross Trophy, edging his suspended teammate Rocket Richard 75 points to 74. Both players had 38 goals to tie for the league lead, but Geoffrion had one more assist to gain the award. In 1960-61 Geoffrion became the second NHL player to score 50 goals in one season.

New York Ranger centre Camille Henry looks for a rebound after taking a shot at Leaf goaltender Harry Lumley. The small forward broke into the NHL in 1953-54 and won the Calder Trophy by scoring 24 goals in 66 games. But then he spent all or parts of the next three seasons in the minors, a strong indicator of how hard it was to make it in the NHL during the 1950s. While at Providence in the AHL, Henry scored 50 goals in 1955-56 and was back on Broadway full-time in 1957-58. He captured his second major award that year, taking home the Lady Byng Trophy while scoring 32 goals for the Rangers. He remained a consistent goal scorer for the remainder of his NHL career (14 years) and once scored four goals in one game against Detroit legend Terry Sawchuk.

STATSBOX

In 1957-58 Camille Henry was the smallest player in the NHL at 151 pounds, while Elmer "Moose" Vasko was the biggest at 210. The average weight of an NHL player in 1996-97 was 198 pounds. The Philadelphia Flyers' six-foot-four superstar Eric Lindros weighs in at 236 pounds.

Unusual Note

Camille Henry once appeared on the game show *To Tell the Truth,* trying to fool the panellists into thinking he had married one of the Dionne quintuplets.

Chicago defenceman Gus Mortson blocks Toronto's Rudy Migay from going after a loose puck while goalie Al Rollins contends with Eric Nesterenko in the crease. On the far left is the other Blackhawk defenceman, Larry Zeidel. Mortson began his career in Toronto where he was paired with Jim Thomson to form a duo that became known as the Gold Dust Twins. After four Stanley Cups in Toronto, Mortson was dealt to Chicago in 1952 where he played for six seasons. An excellent skater who loved body contact, Mortson's game centred on keeping the puck out of his net. His bruising style made him the penalty-minute champ four times but also a first-team all-star in 1949-50. He played his last NHL season with Detroit in 1958-59 and finished with 46 career goals and 1,380 penalty minutes.

TRIVIA

Larry Zeidel began his NHL career with Detroit in 1951-52, winning a Stanley Cup, and moved to Chicago in 1953. He played in 64 games in 1953-54, and then didn't return to the NHL until 1967-68 when the expansion Philadelphia Flyers gave him another chance. He scored two goals in 158 career games.

THE MONEY GAME

When Chicago made the playoffs in 1952-53, the club averaged 11,944 fans per home game. By 1954-55 the Blackhawks had a last-place team and the average dropped to 6,336. In 1955-56 the average went up slightly to 7,431, but the team had to offer specials like three $2.50 seats for the price of two. In 1956-57 the Blackhawks had only 500 season ticket holders and their ticket prices ranged from $4 (for box seats) to $1.25 (second balcony).

Marketing the Game

During the 1920s, when Conn Smythe travelled to many hockey arenas, he found most of them dirty, unclean, and dismal places. The seats were hard and uncomfortable and the dressing rooms were awful. However, while in Winnipeg, he noticed that one arena there was clean and tidy. He vowed to do the same if he ever became involved in a new arena. When he had a strong influence in the building and design of Maple Leaf Gardens, he insisted that it be kept spotless and that the people who entered should feel as if they were going to a hockey palace. Today the building that was opened in 1931 has become antiquated but is still well maintained and is the last of the original six arenas still being used by an NHL team. Chicago, Boston, and Montreal have all built new rinks recently, and Maple Leaf Gardens will be replaced soon. Until a new arena is erected in Toronto, though, Maple Leaf Gardens will remain as a hockey shrine.

By the mid-1950s Maple Leaf founder and owner Conn Smythe was no longer at the centre of the Toronto franchise as he was in this photo on a night when the club paid tribute to goalie Turk Broda. Smythe and a group of investors originally paid $160,000 for the Toronto club in 1927, and he quickly made changes. The nickname was switched from St. Patricks to Maple Leafs because Smythe had worn Maple Leaf badges on his army uniform (he was a veteran of both world wars). The team colours also changed, with blue and white replacing green. Smythe picked those colours because, he said, they represented Canada's blue sky and white snow. During his time at the helm, the Leafs had many great players who became Hall of Fame inductees, including King Clancy, Charlie Conacher, Joe Primeau, Hap Day, Red Horner, Syl Apps, Turk Broda, and Ted Kennedy. By the mid-1950s Smythe was more interested in horse racing and handed control of the Leafs over to first Hap Day and later to his son Stafford. However, he did retain his title of president of the board of directors until he sold his stock in 1961.

Tod Sloan is presented with the J. P. Bickell Trophy, a Toronto team award selected by the board of directors of Maple Leaf Gardens. During the 1950s, the Bickell was given to the Leaf player deemed to be the most valuable to the club. Sloan won the award for his performance in the 1955-56 season when he tied a club record with 37 goals. His 66 points was second best in team history to that date. Quick, with shifty moves, "Slinker" was also an excellent stickhandler. His first full year with the Leafs was in 1950-51 when he tallied 31 goals and 56 points for a Stanley Cup-winning team. He added nine points in 11 playoff games. Before he made it to the big league, Sloan played for the AHL's Pittsburgh and Cleveland teams. It was while he was at Cleveland that Sloan stopped smoking and was able to add the weight he needed to play in the NHL. He played until 1960-61, finishing with a Cup in Chicago, and ended up with 220 goals and 262 assists in 745 games.

TRIVIA

A study of 101 NHL players who played in 1955-56 showed that 65 of them had played in the American Hockey League at some point in their careers, usually in their early years of professional hockey. The study included all six goalies – Jacques Plante, Terry Sawchuk, Harry Lumley, Gump Worsley, Al Rollins, and Glenn Hall – who started for their respective teams. Other names who played in the main developmental league for the NHL included Red Sullivan, Allan Stanley, Sid Smith, Earl Reibel, Jim Thomson, Leo Labine, Bob Goldham, and Fern Flaman. In 1996-97 the AHL was still considered the best league to develop young talent at the professional level. Current prominent graduates include Ken Daneyko, Steve Duchesne, Dino Ciccarelli, Brett Hull, Joe Murphy, Todd Gill, Bernie Nicholls, Steve Thomas, Sylvain Lefebvre, Claude Lemieux, Marty McSorley, and Joel Otto.

THE MONEY GAME

When Toronto owner Conn Smythe heard that his captain was involved in the movement to start a players' association, he called Jim Thomson a traitor. The Leafs sent Thomson to Chicago for a $15,000 waiver fee, and he played there for one season. He was sent back to Toronto but refused to play for the Maple Leafs again and retired at the age of 31. The Leafs had owned and controlled Thomson since the age of 16 when scout Squib Walker signed him in Winnipeg. He helped Toronto win four Stanley Cups and was named captain in 1956, but this distinction earned no loyalty from Smythe. Recently, when the retired NHL players won their pension-surplus lawsuit against the league, the estate of Jim Thomson earned $49,147.95. Later Leaf captains who left the team as a result of money/contract problems include Dave Keon, Darryl Sittler, and Doug Gilmour.

Detroit Red Wing captain Leonard "Red" Kelly takes the ceremonial opening face-off for the 1956-57 season against Maple Leaf captain Jim Thomson. Kelly was the first recipient of the James Norris Trophy in 1953-54 after recording 49 points, including 16 goals, while patrolling the blue line for Detroit. In a defensive era Kelly played a very offensive game for a rear guard, recording nine straight seasons when he scored 10 or more goals. His highest goal-scoring total while playing defence was 19, and he finished in the league's top 10 in scoring three times in the 1950s. By contrast, his main rival, Doug Harvey of the Canadiens, never had a top 10 appearance. In addition to four Stanley Cups with Detroit, Kelly was a six-time first-team all-star. Kelly replaced Ted Lindsay as captain of the Red Wings to start the new season.

Toronto centre Billy Harris scores a goal against Boston goalie Terry Sawchuk. A slick playmaker with an excellent shot, Harris finished his junior career with the Toronto Marlboros by scoring 15 goals and adding 24 assists in 24 playoff games as the Marlies won the Memorial Cup in 1954-55. The Leafs hoped Harris might replace the soon-to-retire Ted Kennedy. He played in 70 games for Toronto in 1955-56, scoring nine times and contributing 13 assists. He spent most of the next season in Rochester in the AHL but also played 23 games for the Leafs and recorded 10 points. The 1957-58 season saw Harris get 16 goals and 28 assists, including his first career hat trick against Boston on October 19, 1957. By 1958-59 Harris was able to establish himself as a Leaf regular and scored 22 goals as the team made the playoffs for the first time in three years.

"Hinky" Harris then added seven points in 12 playoff games.

Marketing the Game

Prior to the 1955-56 season, Maple Leaf Gardens held an open house unveiling new escalators throughout the building. An estimated 20,000 fans turned out, taking tours of the Gardens and getting autographs from Leafs past and present.

Fathers and Sons

Cal Gardner was projected to be a good goal scorer based on his play in the Eastern Hockey League for the New York Rovers. However, he only managed 154 career goals in 11 NHL seasons, scoring more than 20 goals just once. He had two sons who played in the NHL. Dave scored 75 goals and Paul added 201 between 1972 and 1986. All three Gardners played for a combined total of 14 different NHL teams.

Boston Bruin Cal Gardner's stick is stepped on by Toronto's Gord Hannigan as he tries to reach for a loose puck. Gardner began his career with the New York Rangers in the mid-1940s, but his best days were spent with the Maple Leafs between 1948 and 1952. He won the Stanley Cup with Toronto in 1949 and again in 1951. Gardner had his top season in 1950-51 when he scored 23 goals and 51 points for the Leafs. A durable player, the six-foot-one centre once played in 444 consecutive games and moved on to play for Chicago (one season) and Boston (four seasons) in the middle of the streak. After his career ended with 392 points in 696 games, Gardner became a broadcaster with Boston and then with Toronto. His feud with the Canadiens' Ken Reardon is legendary, and Gardner still won't speak to his rival even today.

Boston's Larry Regan (hand on net) tries to dig out the puck with teammate Bob Beckett against a group of Maple Leafs. Regan had quit hockey at the age of 26 to run a gas station. He was tired of playing in the minors and didn't believe he had a chance to make it to the NHL. However, he caught the eye of Boston management, namely Milt Schmidt and Lynn Patrick, with his good stick-handling and playmaking skills. Regan played in 1956-57 for Boston, recording 14 goals and 33 assists in 69 games. It was enough to get him named rookie of the year at the age of 27, but by 1958-59 he was traded to Toronto and reunited with his minor-league coach, Punch Imlach. Regan finished his NHL career with 41 goals and 95 assists in 280 games. In 1990 Sergei Makarov of the Calgary Flames was 31 when he won the Calder Trophy.

STATSBOX

When Larry Regan won the Calder Trophy, he finished with 107 points in the voting. His nearest competitor was Ed Chadwick of Toronto with 85 points. Others who got votes were Billy Dea (Detroit), Forbes Kennedy (Chicago), Pierre Pilote (Chicago), Don Simmons (Boston), Elmer Vasko (Chicago), Jack Bionda (Boston), Barry Cullen (Toronto), and Al MacNeil (Toronto).

Unusual Note

At training camp in 1957 the Boston Bruins became the first club to have a European player try out for an NHL team. Sven "Tumba" Johansson was a member of the Swedish national team. Johansson didn't make the Bruins and returned home. The European invasion didn't really start until another Swede, Borje Salming, made it big in the NHL with the Maple Leafs in 1973.

When Red Sullivan went to New York, Ranger manager Muzz Patrick showed he had great faith in his new centre by giving him sweater number 7. The number had special significance to the Rangers, considering the players who had worn it in the past: Frank Boucher, Phil Watson, and Don Raleigh. After Sullivan the next to wear number 7 was Rod Gilbert. To honour Hall of Famer Gilbert, the Rangers finally retired the number.

Marketing the Game

A total of 67 CBS affiliates decided to pick up NHL games when they went on national television in the United States. The first game was on January 5, 1957, between Chicago and New York. The schedule for that first season included only one game involving a Canadian team (Montreal). Fox Television now has the U.S. national contract, and they don't show any games involving the six Canadian teams.

Chicago goalie Hank Bassen hugs the post against the Maple Leafs' Sid Smith as George "Red" Sullivan stands at the edge of the crease, waiting for a loose puck. Sullivan began his NHL career with the Boston Bruins, playing his first year in 1951-52 and scoring 12 goals in 67 games. Being a red-haired Irishman, Sullivan always wanted to play in Boston, but in 1953-54 he was toiling in the AHL for Hershey where he recorded 119 points. The following year saw Sullivan move to Chicago, and he responded with 19 goals and 61 points. A determined, scrappy hockey player, the centre was traded to the New York Rangers for Wally Hergesheimer. He was nearly killed when speared by the Canadiens' Doug Harvey but recovered and went on to captain and coach the Rangers. Hank Bassen was a feisty goalie known to slash opponents across the leg. After two years in Chicago, Bassen ended up with Detroit in 1960-61. He was in net for the Red Wings when they lost the 1961 final to the Blackhawks. Bassen's nephew Bob currently plays in the NHL with Dallas.

Red Sullivan

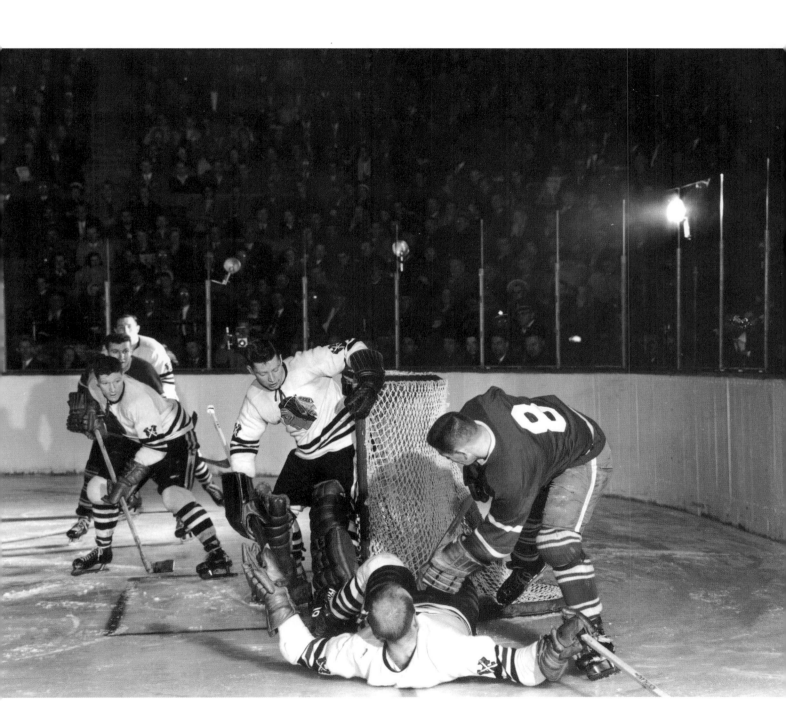

Andy Hebenton of the Rangers puts a shot past Maple Leaf goalie Ed Chadwick. The Toronto goaltender was born with a club foot and, as a youngster, he could only play in goal. After an operation, the foot developed properly as he got older, but he stayed in the net. He first joined the Leafs for five games in 1955-56 when he was called up to replace the injured Harry Lumley. Although he allowed a goal on the first shot he faced (by Bernie Geoffrion), he settled down, allowing only three goals and recording two shutouts. In 1956-57 he played all 70 games for Toronto with five shutouts and a goals-against average of 2.74, but the Leafs missed the playoffs. Toronto finished last in 1957-58, and the following season saw Chadwick's appearances reduced to 31 games. By 1959-60 he was in the minors with Rochester in the AHL.

TRIVIA

Andy Hebenton started a streak of 630 consecutive games played in 1955-56 when he appeared in all 70 games for the Rangers. The streak ended in 1963-64 when Hebenton was with Boston after nine straight seasons of not missing a single game. He never played an NHL game again. Doug Jarvis played in a record 964 consecutive games between 1975 and 1988. Like Hebenton, Jarvis never played another NHL game once the streak was over.

Fathers and Sons

New York general manager Muzz Patrick made Andy Hebenton his first acquisition when he purchased the winger's contract from his father, the legendary Lester Patrick, who was running the Victoria team in the Western Hockey League. Muzz sent $10,000 to his father to complete the deal. In 1997 Chicago general manager Bob Pulford traded his star goalie Ed Belfour to San Jose by dealing with his son-in-law Dean Lombardi, the general manager of the Sharks.

The Maple Leafs and Canadiens are longtime rivals and, as a result, not too many players have appeared on both teams. Only six men who played in both Toronto and Montreal were then elected to the Hockey Hall of Fame: Bert Olmstead, Dickie Moore, Jacques Plante, Frank Mahovlich, Gord Drillon, and George Hainsworth.

THE MONEY GAME

Sponsors have always been important to hockey. In the 1959 playoffs the clock in the Montreal Forum featured an advertisement for Export A cigarettes. In 1997 the Canadian government passed legislation limiting the use of tobacco advertisements. It is believed that this new law will greatly affect tobacco sponsorship of sporting events.

The youngest of eight children, Montreal Canadien winger Dickie Moore broke both legs as a child when he was hit by a car. Fortunately Moore recovered and became what Montreal general manager Frank Selke termed "the best junior in Canada." He made his debut with the Canadiens in 1951-52, recording 33 points in as many games. But then he suffered a serious shoulder injury, and it looked as if he might only be an ordinary NHL player. Still, Moore was highly sought after by teams such as Detroit, New York, and Chicago, but the Canadiens remained patient with their potential star. Once again Moore recovered from his injuries to win two consecutive Art Ross Trophies in 1957-58 (84 points) and 1958-59 (when he set a league record of 96 points). Up to that time only four NHL players had won back-to-back scoring titles (Gordie Howe, Max Bentley, Sweeney Schriner, and Charlie Conacher). Tough and determined, Moore won his first Art Ross playing with a broken wrist for the last part of the season.

Dickie Moore

Marketing the Game

With new coach Howie Meeker on the scene for 1956-57, the Maple Leafs came up with a new slogan that was unveiled at a press conference. "Rock and Roll with Howie Meeker and His Crew Cuts" was the fresh phrase plastered above photographs of Meeker and players Bob Pulford, Bobby Baun, Pat Hannigan, Al MacNeil, and Gary Collins. This was a change from the Leafs' promise in 1955-56 of "Guts, Goals, and Glamour."

STATSBOX

Howie Meeker's tenure as Maple Leaf coach lasted only 70 games, with a winning percentage of .407. Other Leaf coaches who lasted fewer than 100 games are Nick Beverly (17/.588); Joe Crozier (40/.388); Art Duncan (47/.533); George Armstrong (47/.404); Floyd Smith (68/.478); Billy Reay (90/.367); and Doug Carpenter (91/.456).

The Toronto Maple Leafs promoted Howie Meeker to head coach for the 1956-57 season. He had been coaching the Leafs' minor-league team in Pittsburgh and had won a championship in the steel town in 1954-55. Meeker earned $8,000 in his second year in Pittsburgh, and the Leafs gave him a raise to $9,000 to coach the big team. Only 32 himself, Meeker had to work with a very young team that had trouble scoring goals. Meeker ended up with a record of 21-34-14, good for fifth place but well out of the playoffs. The Leaf organization went through major changes before the start of the 1957-58 season, and Meeker wasn't part of the plan, even though he was set to be general manager that year. He didn't see eye to eye with Stafford Smythe and resigned his position with the Leafs.

Howie Meeker

Toronto's Barry Cullen (19) tries to find the puck before goalie Al Rollins of Chicago does, with Blackhawk winger Nick Mickoski, far left, moving in to help out. Like his brother Brian (who played for the Leafs and Rangers from 1954 to 1961), Barry showed great promise as a junior with St. Catharines when the two shared in a Memorial Cup victory in 1953-54. Barry contributed 62 goals and 45 assists for the Teepees that year, and the Leafs assigned him to Winnipeg of the Western Hockey League for the 1955-56 season. After notching 38 goals and 34 assists, he was named rookie of the year in that league. Toronto coach Howie Meeker predicted great things for Cullen, who was noted for his scrappy ability in front of the net. He scored 16 goals for Toronto in his first complete season for the Maple Leafs but was traded to Detroit by 1959-60. He was out of hockey at age 29 and began a successful car dealership.

Fathers and Sons

John Cullen was acquired by the Maple Leafs in 1992-93. Like his father, Barry, he wore number 19. He left the club just two years after he was picked up in a trade with the Hartford Whalers. The final statistics for the Cullen father-and-son tandem as Maple Leafs are: Barry (164 games, 28 goals, 43 assists, 71 points); John (100 games, 26 goals, 45 assists, 71 points).

TRIVIA

Ray Cullen joined the NHL in 1965-66, giving the Cullen family three brothers who had made it to the big league. Ray ended up playing for the New York Rangers, Detroit Red Wings, Minnesota North Stars, and Vancouver Canucks from 1965 to 1971. The Bentleys also had three brothers who played in the NHL: Max, Doug, and Reg. The Sutters hold the record for most brothers in the NHL with six: Darryl, Brian, Duane, Brent, Rich, and Ron.

THE MONEY GAME

Despite winning the Stanley Cup in 1955, Detroit manager Jack Adams made a major deal with the Boston Bruins on June 3 of that year. Terry Sawchuk, Marcel Bonin, Vic Stasiuk, and Lorne Davis went to Boston in exchange for Ed Sanford, Real Chevrefils, Norm Corcoran, Gilles Boisvert, and Warren Godfrey. Adams justified the trade in part by saying he wanted to strengthen the weaker teams. But, in fact, his main goal was to eliminate Terry Sawchuk's big salary (a reported $20,000). Adams only had to pay $10,000 to Glenn Hall, Sawchuk's replacement.

Marketing the Game

For the 1957-58 season the Detroit Red Wings had all their home games shown on local television beginning in the third period. Detroit fans were also able to watch NHL games on CBS on Saturday afternoons and *Hockey Night* in Canada matches on CBC on Saturday night. Jack Adams was concerned about too much hockey on television and contemplated a cutback for the next season. In 1996-97 the Toronto Maple Leafs had 77 of their 82 regular-season games shown on local television.

Detroit goalie Glenn Hall is helped out by Norm Ullman against Toronto's George Armstrong while Warren Godfrey has his eye on the Leafs' Dick Duff. Hall became the Red Wings' regular netminder at the start of the 1955-56 season, replacing the great Terry Sawchuk. His first appearance that year was in the All-Star Game, which was played on October 2 at the Detroit Olympia. The All-Stars, who featured a lineup with a combined 300 goals, could only get one past Hall in a 3-1 Red Wing victory. Ironically Terry Sawchuk played part of the game as a member of the All-Stars. Hall went on to have a great rookie season, winning the Calder Trophy and leading the league with 12 shutouts. Hall had played 103 games as a professional (68 at Indianapolis, 31 at Edmonton, and four at Detroit) before he got his first shutout against Boston during the 1952-53 season when he was called up to replace an injured Sawchuk. After his stint with the Red Wings, Hall played for the Chicago Blackhawks and the St. Louis Blues, racking up 84 shutouts in 18 seasons, which makes him third on the all-time NHL shutout list. In three of his first five NHL seasons Norm Ullman scored more than 20 goals and had a total of 94 by the end of the 1959-60 season. The forward ended his 20-season career in 1974-75 with the Maple Leafs, scoring a total of 490 goals and 739 assists, which still puts him among the NHL's top 25 all-time points leaders.

To help celebrate the club's 75th anniversary in 1985, the Montreal Canadiens announced their all-time dream team as voted by the fans. Five of the players and the coach were prominent in the 1950s. Here is the team: Jacques Plante (goal); Doug Harvey and Larry Robinson (defence); Jean Beliveau (centre); Maurice Richard (right wing); Dickie Moore (left wing); and Toe Blake (coach).

STATSBOX

In 1959-60 Rocket Richard was the NHL's oldest player at 38. Leaf goalie Johnny Bower was next oldest at 35, while Doug Harvey and Ted Lindsay were 34 when the season began. Allan Stanley, Bert Olmstead, and Harry Lumley were each 33.

In 1959-60 Doug Harvey of the Montreal Canadiens won the Norris Trophy (awarded to the NHL's best defenceman) for the fifth time, regaining the honour after teammate Tom Johnson had won it the previous year. The Norris Trophy seemed to be Harvey's personal possession since he won it four times in a row between 1954-55 and 1957-58. Harvey's dominance on the blue line is further evidenced by his eight first-team all-star selections between 1952 and 1960. During this time, the most goals Harvey scored in a season was nine, but he did accumulate 338 assists by the end of the decade. Cool and calm on the ice, Harvey had a style that made him look as if he were uninterested. He excelled at rushing the puck and quarterbacked the Canadiens' devastating power play. For all his talent and awards, Harvey earned $15,000 in 1957-58, a respectable salary in those days. He became captain of the Canadiens when Rocket Richard retired in 1960-61, Harvey's last season in Montreal.

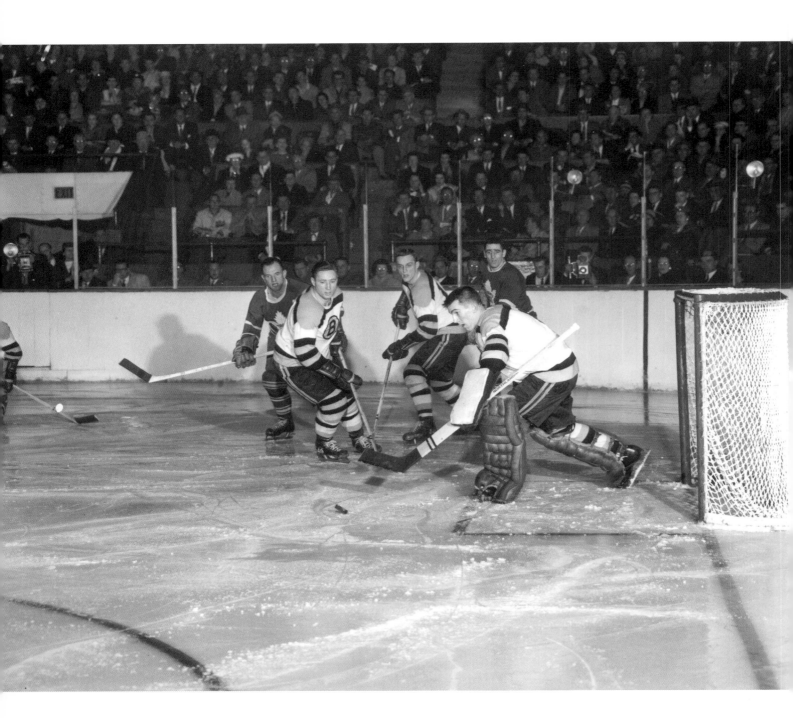

Boston goalie Don Simmons moves to clear a loose puck as teammates Fern Flaman (left) and Doug Mohns keep the Leafs' Ted Kennedy (left) and Sid Smith away from the Bruins' net. Simmons was playing in Springfield of the AHL under coach Eddie Shore when he was called up by the Bruins in 1956-57. Boston needed the left-handed goalie when Norm Defelice proved to be an inadequate replacement for the ill Terry Sawchuk. Simmons made his debut in a nationally televised game against the New York Rangers and lost 5-3. He won the next game 5-2 against Montreal and helped the Bruins knock off Detroit in the playoffs. He didn't play as well in the finals against the Canadiens, but the Bruins turned down a chance to acquire Glenn Hall because of their faith in Simmons. He played in 38 games for Boston in 1957-58, recording five shutouts and taking the Bruins to the finals, only to lose to the Canadiens again.

Unusual Note

Boston goalie Don Simmons was given a two-minute penalty for throwing the puck forward to teammate Jean-Guy Gendron on October 22, 1959, in a game against Detroit. Referee Eddie Powers invoked rule 59(c), a rarely called infraction targeted at goalies who toss the puck too far up the ice, just as Simmons had done. Detroit scored a goal as a result of the two-minute penalty and won the game 4-1.

TRIVIA

Boston traded defenceman Fern Flaman to Toronto in 1950 along with Ken Smith, Leo Boivin, and Phil Maloney in exchange for Bill Ezinicki and Vic Lynn. The Bruins decided they wanted Flaman back and gave the Leafs Dave Creighton in exchange on July 20, 1954. Flaman stayed with Boston until 1960-61 and was eventually elected to the Hall of Fame.

Unusual Note

Voting for major trophies in the 1950s was done on a first-half and second-half total-point basis. When Frank Mahovlich won the Calder, he had 82 first-half points while eventual runner-up Bobby Hull had 39. In the second half Hull out-polled Mahovlich by 77 to 38, but the Leaf winger finished with 120 points and the Blackhawks' rising star had to settle for second with 116.

THE MONEY GAME

Frank Mahovlich pocketed an extra $1,000 when he won the Calder Trophy. In 1996 when Daniel Alfredsson of the Ottawa Senators was named top rookie, he received an extra $10,000. It is interesting to note that Alfredsson also won a close vote over another Blackhawk winger, Eric Daze, 437 points to 416.

The Toronto Maple Leafs eagerly awaited the arrival of Frank Mahovlich ever since he scored five goals in his first two games for St. Michael's of the Ontario Hockey Association when he was just 16. The Leafs brought him up to the big club in 1956-57 to play three games late in March. He scored his first NHL goal against Detroit on March 24, 1957, at the Olympia. The following season, 1957-58, he won the Calder Trophy with 20 goals and 36 points while playing centre. He was then shifted to left wing and notched 22 goals in 1958-59 and 11 points in 12 playoff games that year. By the end of his third season, Mahovlich had scored 61 times. In comparison, the great Gordie Howe only tallied 35 times in his first three years.

Frank Mahovlich

Bobby Hull was 13 when he was first noticed by Chicago scout Bob Wilson. The Blackhawks controlled Hull as soon as Wilson put the youngster on the team's protected list. Blessed with dazzling speed and an incredible physique, Hull became, at 18, the youngest player ever to wear a Chicago uniform when he started the 1957-58 season. He scored his first goal on October 22, 1957, against Don Simmons of the Boston Bruins. As a rookie, he scored 13 goals and followed that with 18 in his second season. By his third year in the NHL, Hull led the league in goals with 39 (tied with the Bruins' Bronco Horvath) and in points with 81.

STATSBOX

Bobby Hull and Frank Mahovlich were often compared to each other when they were both rookies in 1957-58. The previous season, 1956-57, Hull scored 33 goals with St. Catharines of the Ontario Hockey Association, while Mahovlich (a year older than Hull) had 52 with St. Michael's. The "Big M" outscored Hull (20 to 13) in their first year in the NHL, but the "Golden Jet" finished his career with 610 goals to 533 for Mahovlich. Both men also played in the World Hockey Association where Hull outscored Mahovlich 346 to 93.

TRIVIA

Bobby Hull never played a single game in the minor leagues before he joined the Chicago Blackhawks. However, he did play as a junior in four Ontario cities – Belleville, Hespeler, Woodstock, and St. Catharines – before he made it to the Windy City.

Andy Bathgate was the last player to win the Hart Trophy (1958-59) on a team that didn't make the playoffs. The fifth-place Rangers lost out on post-season play by losing their last game to the Montreal Canadiens. Bathgate had an outstanding year with 40 goals and 48 assists and a third-place finish in the scoring race. Chicago goalie Al Rollins also won the league's MVP award in the 1950s (1953-54) when his team finished out of the playoffs and in sixth place.

THE MONEY GAME

In 1955, 23-year-old Andy Bathgate upset Phil Watson, his New York Ranger coach, by showing up late at training camp in a $4,500 sports car.

From the time he was 16 and watched New York train in his native Winnipeg, Andy Bathgate wanted to be a Ranger. He admired New York stars such as Alex Shibicky, Neil Colville, and Bryan Hextall. Bathgate joined the Rangers' junior affiliate in Guelph, Ontario, and captained the Biltmores to the Memorial Cup in 1952. He spent the next two seasons dividing his time between the minors and the Rangers before staying with New York for good in 1955-56. In his first full year on Broadway, Bathgate had 20 goals and 20 assists. He began his career wearing sweater number 14 but switched to number 9 when it became available in 1956, perhaps hoping the success of Gordie Howe, Rocket Richard, and Ted Kennedy would be his, too. It must have worked: Bathgate went on to score a total of 349 goals and 624 assists in 17 seasons.

Lorne "Gump" Worsley stops a shot from Maple Leaf Tod Sloan. Worsley began his NHL career with the New York Rangers in 1952-53 when he played in 50 games, recording two shutouts and a 3.06 goals-against average. But he was replaced by Johnny Bower the following year only to regain his job in 1954-55. Three seasons later Worsley was once again in the minors but returned to New York when no suitable replacement was found.

Although Worsley had a great glove hand and a respectable goals-against average, Ranger coach Phil Watson wasn't a fan. Watson accused Worsley of having a beer belly, which was denied by Gump, who insisted he was a strict rye drinker. Worsley remained a Ranger until 1963 when he was traded to Montreal. He finished his 21-season career with the Minnesota North Stars in 1973-74.

Marketing the Game

Gump Worsley made an appearance on *The Steve Allen Show* in New York in 1955. His guest spot was scheduled after a Ranger game, but Worsley was reluctant to appear because he was tired and had to travel to Boston for a game the next night. However, Worsley did go on the show at about 12:45 a.m. He didn't get home until 3:00 a.m. and had to take a 7:00 a.m. train to Boston. Even though Worsley felt sick, he shut out the Bruins 4-0. During the 1960s, the Rangers' Ed Giacomin and Bernie Geoffrion were on *The Tonight Show* with Johnny Carson. In June 1994 the Rangers' Mark Messier, Brian Leetch, and Mike Richter brought the Stanley Cup along when they visited David Letterman.

THE MONEY GAME

Bill Hay was teamed with left winger Bobby Hull and right winger Murray Balfour to form what Chicago coach Rudy Pilous termed the "Million Dollar Line." Pilous insisted that even a million dollars wouldn't be enough for the trio. It is interesting to note that Hay was purchased from Montreal for $25,000 while Balfour was also bought from the Canadiens for $20,000. Both transactions were completed in 1959.

Unusual Note

"I have urged increased calling of restraining fouls like hooking, tripping, and elbowing." The author of this statement wasn't a current NHL leader such as Gary Bettman or Brian Burke. The speaker was NHL president Clarence Campbell, who made the remark during the 1959-60 season. He further added that the highly skilled players in the league weren't allowed to perform their artistry because of other players who refused to follow the rules.

Chicago's Bill "Red" Hay (11) stands his ground in front of the New York Ranger net. Hay's route to the NHL differed from those of most players in the 1950s. He first attended the University of Saskatchewan for two years before going to Colorado College in the United States where he earned a bachelor of science degree in geology. Hay became the first American college-trained player to win the Calder Trophy as the NHL's best rookie for 1959-60. He scored 18 goals and 37 assists for the Blackhawks, who had purchased his rights from the Montreal Canadiens.

Bill Hay

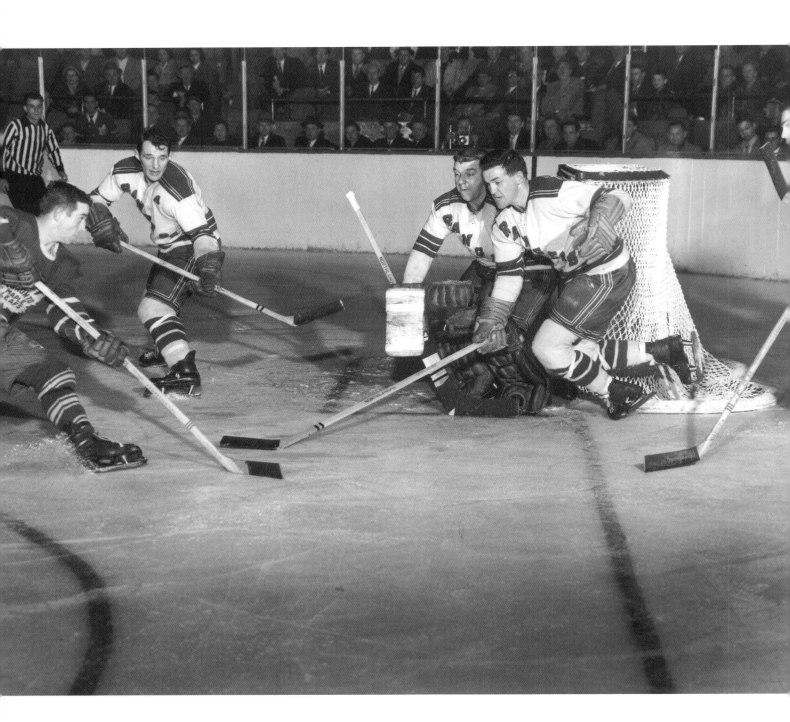

New York defenceman Jack Evans (*right*) is about to take a run at the Leafs' Dick Duff while goalie Gump Worsley and Bill Gadsby (*A* on sweater) look to stop any scoring attempt. A native of Wales, Evans played with the Rangers between 1948 and 1958 and was known as a solid defender. Basically shy and quiet, he displayed raw power and had three seasons of more than 100 penalty minutes while in New York. Evans killed penalties and worked on the power play, although his highest point total with the Rangers was 12. In 1958 he moved to Chicago and helped the Blackhawks win the Stanley Cup in 1961. When his career was over, Evans turned to coaching and handled NHL teams such as Cleveland and California. He had some success with the Hartford Whalers and still holds the club record for coaching wins at 163. In the 1986 playoffs Evans and the Whalers took the eventual champion Montreal Canadiens to a seventh game before losing in overtime on a Claude Lemieux goal.

STATSBOX

Defenceman Bill Gadsby achieved a Ranger club record by scoring 14 goals in 1957-58, breaking Earl Seibert's mark for New York rear guards of 13 set in 1933-34. In 1958-59 Gadsby set an NHL record for defencemen by recording 46 assists, passing Doug Harvey's mark of 44. Gadsby got the assist to earn the new record on the last Saturday of the season on a goal by Andy Hebenton in a game the Rangers had to win to make the playoffs. The Rangers won that game but lost the next and missed the postseason in 1959.

Marketing the Game

On December 2, 1956, just after a Leafs-Rangers contest, several New York Rangers appeared on live television in a show called *Omnibus*. The players demonstrated hockey skills like stickhandling, shooting, and the defensive aspects of the game. Andy Bathgate shot a puck at a car, making a number of dents in order to impress the American audience with the force of the hard rubber disk. The demonstration was staged to preview NHL games that were to be televised nationally on CBS beginning in January 1957.

STATSBOX

Between November 1 and 29, 1959, the Canadiens won 10 games and tied one, all with Plante wearing the mask. He had two shutouts during this stretch. The Maple Leafs finally beat Plante 1-0 on December 2 on a goal by Frank Mahovlich. Toe Blake asked Plante not to wear the mask for a game against Detroit on March 8. The Canadiens lost 3-0, and Plante put the mask back on for good, starting with a 9-4 win over Toronto in his next game. The cost of Plante's first mask was $7.50.

Unusual Note

During the 1950s, NHL teams generally carried only one goalie (to save on one big-league salary), and if the starter was injured on the road, the home team provided a "house" goalie as a replacement. The Canadiens didn't like this arrangement very much and, in 1959, they signed Montreal sports columnist Jacques Beauchamp as the alternate goalie for road games. Not too talented and generally out of condition for the rigours of the NHL, Beauchamp was quite willing but never did get into a game.

Although Jacques Plante was the first goalie to win the Vezina Trophy five times in a row, the Canadien netminder is best remembered for introducing the mask as a regular piece of goaltender equipment. Tired of broken noses, cheekbone fractures, and other facial injuries, Plante had been using a small mask in practice and wanted to wear it during a game. He got support from NHL president Clarence Campbell, but not from his own coach, Toe Blake. That changed on the night of November 1, 1959, when Plante took an Andy Bathgate shot in the face during a game at Madison Square Garden. The game was held up while Plante received stitches, and the goaltender made it clear to Blake that he wouldn't return to the net without his mask. After seeing the mess Bathgate's shot had made of Plante's face, Blake relented and gave his permission. The Canadiens won the game 3-1, and hockey would never look the same again. Note in the photograph how small Plante's gloves and pads are compared to a modern goalie's.

New York Ranger defenceman Lou Fontinato, far left, moves in on the Maple Leafs' Gerry James while goalie Gump Worsley tries to find the puck between his pads. In his first full year in the NHL, 1955-56, Fontinato set a league record with 202 penalty minutes in 70 games. He also added three goals and 15 assists but was mostly known for his toughness. On January 11, 1956, Fontinato caught Rocket Richard with a punch over the eye that quickly ended a fight between the two. The one-punch knockout of Richard gave Fontinato the reputation he was looking for – heavyweight champion of the NHL. Gordie Howe, however, terminated that title in a much-celebrated 1959 fight with "Leapin' Louie."

Unusual Note

Lou Fontinato wanted to be known as a tough guy, but he cared about what his mother thought. After being cut for 12 stitches behind the ear by a high stick, Fontinato didn't want to wear any bandages on his head because the game was on national television and he worried about what his mother would think. Only when told that broadcaster Bud Palmer would assure the audience that Fontinato wasn't seriously hurt did the Ranger defenceman agree to put on the bandages and return to the game.

THE MONEY GAME

Gerry James played 11 seasons for the Winnipeg Blue Bombers of the Canadian Football League between 1952 and 1963. An all-star running back, James also played for the Maple Leafs for parts of four seasons between 1955 and 1960. He felt that hockey wasn't as rough as football, but he decided to leave the Leafs and hockey when he was fined $100 for poor play such as "failing to take his man out."

Hector "Toe" Blake gives direction to his two greatest stars, Jean Beliveau and captain Maurice Richard. Blake brought his tremendous work ethic and a high level of intensity to a team loaded with talent. His blue-collar approach was gained while he worked in the mines or in construction during his summers as an NHL player. He was able to stay in great shape and loved the discipline of the 7:00 a.m. whistle. He played in the NHL until the age of 36 and would have lasted longer if a broken leg hadn't halted his career. Blake started his coaching career with the Houston Huskies of the United States Hockey League before moving to the AHL's Buffalo Bisons, then finished his minor-league stint with Valleyfield of the Quebec Hockey League. He was given the Montreal job on June 8, 1955, beating out two other candidates, Billy Reay and Roger Leger.

TRIVIA

Toe Blake won the Stanley Cup as a rookie coach in 1955-56. He set a standard that was followed by Claude Ruel (1968-69), Al MacNeil (1970-71), and Jean Perron (1985-86), who also won hockey's most coveted prize in their first year behind the Canadien bench. Jacques Demers (1992-93) also won the Cup in his first year with the Canadiens, but unlike the others, he had coached in the NHL previously.

STATSBOX

Between 1956 and 1960 the Canadiens won five straight Stanley Cups. During that time, Toe Blake's playoff coaching record was 40 wins and nine defeats.

Toe Blake

TRIVIA

Jean Beliveau became the first hockey player to appear on the cover of *Sports Illustrated* on January 23, 1956. During the 1950s, Ted Lindsay, Gordie Howe, Jacques Plante, and Andy Bathgate also appeared on the cover of the prestigious magazine.

THE MONEY GAME

For his superb 1955-56 season, Jean Beliveau received the following bonus money from the league: $1,000 for the Hart Trophy; $1,000 for the Art Ross Trophy; $1,000 for being on the team that finished first; $1,000 for winning the semifinal round; $1,000 for winning the Stanley Cup; and $1,000 as a first-team all-star. He also got $2,000 from Canadien management, matching the amount from the league for the trophies.

The Montreal Canadiens' Jean Beliveau is surrounded by four Maple Leafs in front of the Toronto net. Beliveau was in a great bargaining position when he signed his first contract with Montreal. He had scored 50 goals in 1952-53 for the Quebec Aces of the Quebec Senior Hockey League. That feat earned him a salary of $20,000 per season, an unheard of sum at the time. Beliveau didn't enjoy a great rookie season due to injuries, but he rebounded with 37 goals in his second year. Beliveau's first big season was 1955-56 when he led the league in goals (47) and points (88). He also played a physical game, with 143 minutes in penalties. Along with the Art Ross Trophy, Beliveau also won the Hart Trophy as the league's most valuable player. In the 1956 playoffs Beliveau tied a record by scoring 12 goals in the postseason. Seven of the goals came in the finals against Detroit when Montreal captured the Stanley Cup. In 1958-59 Beliveau set a new mark for centremen with 91 points.

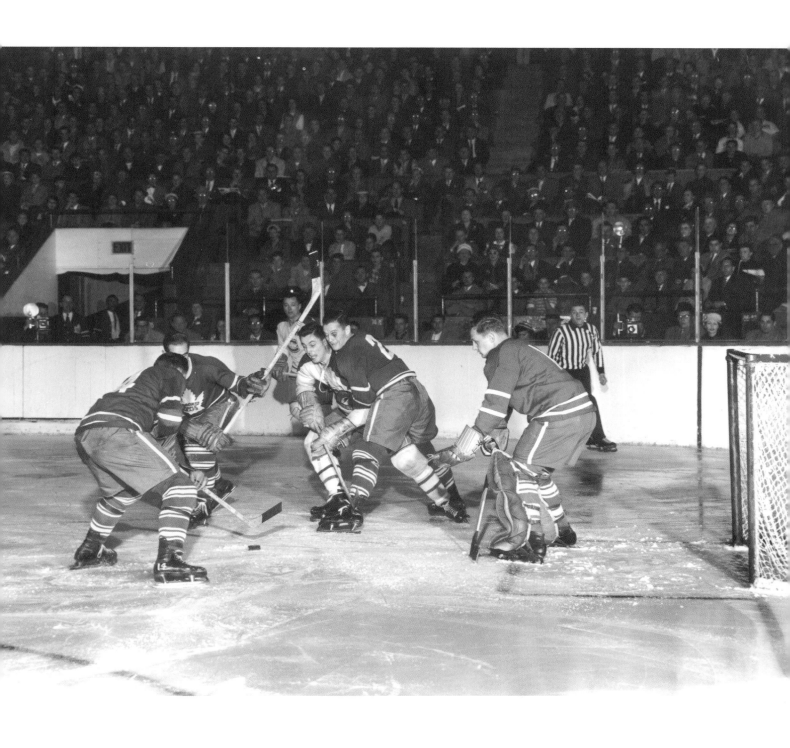

Jack Adams (seated in the front row wearing a bow tie) was the general manager of the Detroit Red Wings from 1927 to 1947 and was involved in all seven Detroit Red Wing Stanley Cup victories between 1936 and 1955. Included in his record are seven straight first-place finishes from 1948-49 to 1954-55. As a player, Adams had enjoyed Cup wins with the Toronto Arenas in 1918 and the Ottawa Senators in 1927. Despite his great success, Adams wasn't well liked and could be a mean and vindictive man when he felt the urge. He showed no loyalties and traded away many great players from the Red Wing championship teams. Here he is pictured with the 1955-56 Red Wings, a team that started the season with only nine players from the club that had won the Cup the previous spring. Gordie Howe is in the second row, third from the left. Adams grew to hate Ted Lindsay (*C* on sweater) so much that he lied to the press about Lindsay's salary. The Detroit autocrat faked a contract that showed Lindsay earning $25,000 when, in reality, he was earning $12,000 at the time. By 1958-59 the Red Wings finished last mostly due to Adams's poor trades.

TRIVIA

The 1955-56 Detroit Red Wings featured three rookies who would become members of the Hall of Fame: goalie Glenn Hall (seated in the front row), Johnny Bucyk (second row, second from left), and Norm Ullman (in the centre of the third row).

Unusual Note

The NHL management during the 1950s expected every player to keep his mind and body on the game only. Jack Adams, for instance, didn't want his Red Wings to overindulge in sexual activity, which he felt would hinder their concentration on hockey. He pleaded with his players to abstain and wasn't above digging up information from a variety of sources to confirm any suspicions. These edicts didn't just apply to single players but those who were married, as well. Essentially wives weren't welcome and getting hitched during the season was severely frowned upon. Nick Mickoski, an NHL player with New York and Chicago during the 1950s, must have bought into the brainwashing when he declared at the age of 28 that love and marriage would have to wait until his hockey career was over. In December 1957 Adams made a deal with the Blackhawks to acquire Mickoski.

Unusual Note

The Toronto Maple Leafs quickly realized the importance of a quality farm system, just as their former employee Frank Selke had. The Leafs and Canadiens shared responsibility for the Rochester Americans of the AHL during the 1950s. By 1959 the Leafs took over complete control of the Americans, which became Toronto's top farm team for many years. Today the Rochester Americans still play in the AHL (as the Buffalo Sabres' top affiliate), while the Leafs' main farm club is located in St. John's, Newfoundland. The Canadiens' development squad is now found in Fredericton, New Brunswick.

THE MONEY GAME

Just about all NHL players had off-season jobs during the 1950s. Many of the 1958 Stanley Cup champion Montreal Canadiens had sales jobs in the summer, including Jacques Plante (cars), Doug Harvey (aluminum windows), Phil Goyette (furniture), Don Marshall (beer), and Henri Richard (oil).

The architect of the 1957-58 Stanley Cup champion Montreal Canadiens was Frank Selke, Sr., seated in the front row, third from the left, between Toe Blake and Rocket Richard. A quiet, soft-spoken gentleman with superb planning skills, Selke came to the Canadiens in 1946 after gaining 20 years of experience with the Maple Leafs as Conn Smythe's right-hand man. By sponsoring a variety of teams in Canada and the United States, the Canadiens built the most productive farm system in hockey. The 1958 Cup winners featured farm products such as Jacques Plante (front row, far left), Tom Johnson, Dickie Moore (second row, second from left), Henri Richard (third row, second from left), Dollard St. Laurent, Claude Provost, Phil Goyette, Don Marshall, Bob Turner, Jean-Guy Talbot, Andre Pronovost, Bernie Geoffrion (second row, second from right), and Jean Beliveau (second row, middle).

George "Punch" Imlach sits in the middle of the first row in the Maple Leafs' team photograph at the start of the 1959-60 season. Imlach joined the Leafs in August, 1958 as assistant general manager. An experienced minor-league coach who had never missed the playoffs, Imlach quickly came to dislike Leaf coach Billy Reay's coaching style. When he was promoted to general manager, Imlach fired Reay and sought to sign Alf Pike (with Winnipeg in the Western Hockey League) to coach the Leafs. But when he couldn't come to terms with Pike, Imlach named himself coach and Bert Olmstead as his playing assistant. Not lacking in ego or gumption, Imlach boldly predicted the Leafs would make the playoffs despite a horrific start in 1958-59. A miracle finish saw the Leafs grab the fourth and final playoff position on the last night of the season. From then on there was no doubt about who was running the Maple Leafs.

TRIVIA

The 1959-60 team photograph features a number of Leafs who were with the Toronto club when it won three Stanley Cups in a row between 1962 and 1964: front row: Ron Stewart, George Armstrong, Tim Horton, Johnny Bower; second row: Bob Pulford, Bert Olmstead, Billy Harris, Dick Duff; third row: Allan Stanley, Frank Mahovlich; fourth row: Carl Brewer, Bobby Baun, Gerry Ehman. Red Kelly was added to the team on February 10, 1960.

STATSBOX

Prior to the start of the 1959-60 season, Maple Leaf coach and general manager Punch Imlach predicted his team would get 75 points (in a 70-game schedule). The team ended up with 79 and second place. Prior to the start of the 1996-97 season, Leaf president and general manager Cliff Fletcher predicted the team would get 90 points (in an 82-game schedule). The team finished with 68 and was 23rd out of 26 teams.

Afterword

As the bell sounded in Maple Leaf Gardens to end the fourth and final game, Montreal goaltender Jacques Plante took off his mask and held it high, as if to say, "There, I told you so." Plante and the Canadiens had just swept the Maple Leafs in the 1960 finals, winning the last game 4-0. The use of a mask by "Jake the Snake" was vindicated, and his defiance of the NHL coaching fraternity proved that some players were determined to protect themselves on and off the ice.

On-ice changes soon to be ushered in were the implementation of backup goalies on the bench during games, better protection for goaltenders (pads, gloves), and the use of helmets, which initially were severely frowned upon. Off-ice changes saw the rebirth of Ted Lindsay's players' association, this time permanently, and the use of agents to look after the best interests of the players, not the owners. Some of these reforms would happen gradually, but Plante's action led the way and demonstrated what could be accomplished if players stood up to management.

The game was also changing, as it still does today, because of television. *Hockey Night in Canada* made Saturday night even more magical for Canadians from coast to coast because now they could actually see their heroes. People no longer huddled around the radio; they now gathered around the television set, even if it did have a wobbly black-and-white picture. Canadians no longer had to imagine what Foster Hewitt was describing; they could actually witness the events themselves. While no picture could ever match what the imagination made of Hewitt's "He shoots! He scores!", television brought players closer to the fans. Hockey legends were now in our living rooms to stay.

In 1957 in the United States CBS began to broadcast hockey on a national basis, introducing the game to millions who had never known it before. This event, in turn, started the grass-roots movement toward NHL expansion, which predominantly occurred in the United States, especially in the early years. Today Fox Television, and ESPN to a lesser degree, have taken over as the main national television broadcasters of hockey in the United States. The messenger and message may have changed since 1957, but the importance of television in developing the world's fastest game is still the same.

The impact of the Montreal Canadiens' dynasty would fade after the Habs' fifth Stanley Cup victory. The team would have no Stanley Cup wins during the first four years of the 1960s, although it would finish first three times during this "famine." The new power would be the Toronto Maple Leafs, a team that hadn't won a Cup since the Barilko goal of 1951. By 1959 Toronto had turned the corner, and although the Leafs had suffered two consecutive defeats at the hands of the Canadiens in the finals, they were poised to start their own dynasty.

By 1965 the Canadiens had found the missing spark and started another run of Stanley Cup wins, ending in 1969. Canada's centennial year, 1967, saw hockey's greatest rivalry have one more shining moment when the Leafs won their last Cup to date, defeating the Canadiens in a match-up made in heaven. Together Toronto and Montreal combined for nine Stanley Cups, starting in 1960, with only Chicago breaking the string in 1961.

Although the 1960s brought a new group of players into the NHL, many of the stars of the 1950s were still going strong in the new decade. Jean Beliveau, Jacques Plante, Glenn Hall, Bobby Hull, Gordie Howe, Gump Worsley, George Armstrong, Tim Horton, and Frank Mahovlich had great moments not only in the 1950s but also in the 1960s and even into the 1970s. The 1950s produced a skilled, tough, courageous, determined, and long-lasting group of players. All of them had the hearts of champions, which is probably why many of them are in the Hockey Hall of Fame where their achievements in the game we knew are recorded for all time.

ACKNOWLEDGMENTS

The author wishes to thank Gino
Granieri, Paul Patskou, and Scott Hardy
for their research materials. A thank you
to Patricia Stevens, who prepared the
manuscript. Many thanks to my editor,
Michael Carroll, who championed the
idea at Raincoast Books. A special thank
you to my wife, Maria Leonetti, for all
her help, understanding,
and support.